THE GREAT INFLUENZA

THE **GREAT INFLUENZA**

The True Story of the Deadliest Pandemic in History

JOHN M. BARRY
Adapted by Catherine S. Frank

VIKING

VIKING
An imprint of Penguin Random House LLC, New York

First published in the United States of America by Viking,
an imprint of Penguin Random House LLC, 2024

Adapted from *The Great Influenza: The Story of the Deadliest Plague in History*,
copyright © 2004 by John M. Barry

Visit us online at PenguinRandomHouse.com.

Library of Congress Cataloging-in-Publication Data is available.

ISBN 9780593404690

1st Printing

Printed in the United States of America

LSCH

Design by Anabeth Bostrup

Text set in Baskerville

To my darling Anne
and to the spirit that was Paul Lewis

CONTENTS

Part IV: Deadly Decisions

Part V: After 1918

THE GREAT
INFLUENZA

— + —

Prologue

In 1918 an influenza virus emerged—probably in the United States—that would spread around the world. Before that worldwide pandemic faded away in 1920, it would kill more people than any other outbreak of disease in human history. The bubonic plague in the 1300s, often called the black death, killed a far larger proportion of the population, but in raw numbers the influenza killed more than plague did then and more than AIDS has since its appearance in the early 1980s.

The lowest estimate of the pandemic's worldwide death toll is twenty-one million, in a world with a population less than one-third of today's. That estimate comes from a study of the disease at the time that it was happening, and newspapers have often cited it since, but it is almost certainly wrong. Epidemiologists today estimate that the influenza likely caused at least fifty million deaths worldwide, and possibly as many as one hundred million. That was around 5 percent of the world's population at the time.

Normally influenza chiefly kills the elderly and infants, but in the 1918 pandemic roughly half of those who died were young men and women in the prime of their lives, in their twenties and thirties. Yet the story of the 1918 influenza virus is not simply one of havoc, death, and desolation. Nor is it merely a story of society fighting a war against nature while simultaneously fighting a world war.

It is also a story of science and discovery. Of how people think and how to change the way people think. And of how, amid near-utter chaos, a few people were able to find the utter calm needed to plan grim, determined action.

In the United States particularly, the story is one of a handful of extraordinary people. These were men and some very few women who developed the fundamental science upon which much of today's medicine is based, including vaccines, antitoxins, and techniques still in use.

In a way, these researchers had spent much of their lives preparing for the confrontation that occurred in 1918. Throughout history, war had often spread disease. And so the leaders of American medical research had anticipated that a major epidemic of some kind might erupt during the Great War (now known as World War I).

This story, however, begins earlier. Before medicine could confront this disease with any promise of effect, it had to become scientific. It had to be revolutionized.

Medicine is not yet and may never be an exact science—the quirks of individual patients and doctors may prevent that—but up to a few decades before World War I, the practice of medicine had remained almost unchanged from more than two thousand years earlier. Then, in Europe, medical science changed and, finally, the practice of medicine changed, too.

But even after European medicine changed, medicine in the United States did not. In research and education especially, American medicine lagged far behind.

Not until very late in the nineteenth century did a virtual handful of leaders in American medical science begin a revolution that transformed American medicine from the most backward in the developed world into the best in the world.

Shortly before the Great War began in 1914, the people who so wanted to transform American medicine succeeded. They created a system that could produce people capable of thinking in a new way, capable of challenging existing systems. They, together with the first generation of scientists they had trained, stood on alert, hoping against but expecting and preparing for the eruption of an epidemic.

When it came, they placed their lives in the path of the disease and applied all their knowledge and powers to defeat it. As it overwhelmed them, they concentrated on constructing the body of knowledge necessary to eventually triumph. The scientific knowledge that ultimately came out of the influenza pandemic pointed directly—and still points—to much that lies in medicine's future.

PART I

BEFORE

CHAPTER ONE

~ଓଚ୍ଚ

A Revolution from Nothing

The two most important questions in science are "What can I know?" and "How can I know it?"

And the way one goes about answering these questions, one's methodology, matters as much as the questions themselves. How one pursues a question often determines, or at least affects, the answer. Indeed, methodology, what we call the scientific method, matters more than anything else. Testing a prediction or hypothesis—a theory that says "If this, then that"—is the single most important element of modern methodology.

But what you may know as the scientific method has not always been used by those who inquire into nature. Through most of known history, investigators trying to understand the natural world, to penetrate what we call science, relied upon reason alone. They based their thinking mostly on observation and did not probe nature through experiments. This commitment to logic was actually problematic for science in general and medicine in particular, because if you don't test your hypothesis, any progress is coincidental. If you *do* test your hypothesis, then progress is inevitable. And for the bulk of twenty-five hundred years, the actual treatment of patients by physicians made almost no progress at all.

It took until the nineteenth century before that finally began to change—and then it changed with extraordinary rapidity. Medicine began to make use of objective measurements and mathematics. For two millennia physicians' senses had mattered far more than any objective measurement, so they had always avoided applying mathematics to the study of the body or disease. It was only in the 1820s that French clinicians began using thermometers—two hundred years *after* they had been invented. Nineteenth-century clinicians also began taking advantage of methods discovered in the 1700s to measure other bodily functions precisely.

By then in Paris, a man named Pierre Louis had taken an even more significant step. Using the most basic mathematical analysis— nothing more than arithmetic—he studied how the different treatments patients received for the same disease related to the results. For the first time in history, a physician was correlating data and creating a reliable and systematic database. Physicians could have done this earlier. It required only taking careful notes. Yet this was the point when modern medicine diverged from the previous two thousand years.

Louis compared treatments with results to reach a conclusion about a treatment's effectiveness—based on data, he rejected bleeding, or removing blood from patients intentionally, as a useless therapy, for example. He and others also used autopsies to correlate the condition of organs with symptoms. They dissected organs and compared diseased organs to healthy ones. What they found was astounding and compelling, and it helped lead to a new conception of disease as something that invaded parts of the body. This was a fundamental first step in what would become a revolution.

Louis's influence could not be overstated. Nor could that of what became known as "the numerical system," which included advances such as the stethoscope, the laryngoscope, the ophthalmoscope, the measurements of temperature and blood pressure, and the study of parts of the body. These advances created distance between the doctor and the patient, as well as between the patient and disease. They turned the human body into an object that could be studied. These steps had to come to make progress in medicine.

In England in the 1840s and 1850s, an epidemiologist named John Snow began applying mathematics in a new way. Epidemiologists investigate patterns of disease with the goal of preventing community spread and future outbreaks. Snow had made meticulous observations of the patterns of a cholera outbreak, noting who got sick and who did not, where the sick lived and how they lived, and where the healthy lived and how they lived. He tracked down the disease to a contaminated well in London. He concluded that contaminated water caused the disease. It was brilliant detective work, brilliant epidemiology.

Snow needed no scientific knowledge, no laboratory findings, to reach his conclusions. Like Pierre Louis's correlation of treatments with results, his work could have been conducted a century earlier or ten centuries earlier. But his work reflected a new way of looking at the world, a new way of seeking explanations, a new methodology, a new use of mathematics as an analytical tool.

Medicine was advancing by borrowing from other sciences. And when investigators began using a magnificent new tool—a microscope equipped with a new kind of lens, which came into use in the 1830s—an even wider universe began to open.

Never had there been a time so exciting in medicine.

Still, with the exception of these findings on cholera and similar findings on typhoid, little of this new scientific knowledge could be translated into curing or preventing disease. And much of what was being discovered was not understood because physicians were not receiving the right education.

By the 1870s, European medical schools required rigorous scientific training. In contrast, most American medical schools were owned by a faculty whose profits and salaries were paid by student fees. The schools often had no admission standards other than the ability to pay tuition. No medical school in America allowed students to either perform autopsies or see patients routinely, and medical education often consisted of nothing more than two four-month terms of lectures. Few medical schools had any association with a university, and fewer still had ties to a hospital. Even at Harvard University, a medical student could fail four of nine courses and still get a medical degree in 1870.

This began to change in 1873, when an American man named

Johns Hopkins died, leaving behind $3.5 million to found a university and hospital. It was at the time the most significant gift ever given to a university. The trustees of Hopkins's estate, against the advice of leading university presidents, decided to model Johns Hopkins University after the greatest German universities, places where people were consumed with creating new knowledge, not simply teaching what was believed.

The trustees made this decision precisely because there was no such university in America and they recognized the need. A board member later explained, "There was a strong demand, among the young men of this country, for opportunities to study beyond the ordinary courses of a college or a scientific school . . . The strongest evidence of this demand was the increased attendance of American students upon lectures of German universities."[1] The trustees decided that quality would sell. They intended to hire only excellent professors and provide opportunities for advanced study.

Their plan was in many ways an entirely American ambition: to create a revolution from nothing. It made little sense to locate the new institution in Baltimore, Maryland, a squalid industrial and port city. Unlike Philadelphia, Boston, or New York, Baltimore had no tradition of supporting charitable causes, no social elite ready to lead, and certainly no intellectual tradition. Even the architecture of Baltimore seemed exceptionally dreary: long lines of row houses crowding against the street and yet almost no street life or community—the people of Baltimore seemed to live inward, in backyards and courtyards.

In fact, there was no base whatsoever upon which to build . . . except the money Hopkins had left.

The Hopkins opened in 1876. Its medical school would not open until 1893, but it succeeded so brilliantly and quickly that by the outbreak of World War I in 1914 American medical science had caught up to Europe and was about to surpass it. By then, those trained directly or indirectly by the Hopkins were already leading the world in investigating pneumonia. They could in some instances prevent and cure it. And their story begins with one man.

CHAPTER TWO

~~~

The Modernization of American Medicine

William Henry Welch was born in 1850 in Norfolk, Connecticut, a small town in the northern part of the state that remains even today a hilly and wooded retreat. His grandfather, great-uncle, father, and four uncles were all physicians. Yet it was not always clear that Welch would become a physician too.

Welch's mother died when he was six months old. His sister, three years older, was sent away, and his father was distant both emotionally and physically. His childhood was marked by what would become a pattern throughout his life: loneliness masked by social activity. Welch charmed without effort. He inspired without effort. There was something about him that made others want him to think well of them. A later age would call this "charisma." And yet he tended not to return the feelings of attachment so many felt toward him.

He attended Yale University, and he graduated third in his

class. With his family pressuring him to become a physician, Welch returned to Norfolk and apprenticed to his father. It was an old-fashioned practice. Nothing his father did reflected any knowledge of the newest medical concepts. Like most American physicians, his father ignored objective measurements such as temperature and blood pressure, and he even mixed prescriptions without measuring dosages, often relying on taste. This apprenticeship was not a happy time for Welch. In his own later accounts of his training, he passed over it as if it had never occurred. But sometime during it, his views of medicine changed.

At some point he decided that if he was going to become a physician, he would do so in his own way. At the time, those preparing for medicine apprenticed for six months or a year and then attended medical school. Welch had served his apprenticeship. But in the next step he took, he marked out a new course. Welch returned to school all right—to study chemistry.

Not only did no medical school in the United States require entering students to have any scientific knowledge or a college degree, neither did any American medical school emphasize science. Far from it. To Welch, however, chemistry seemed to be a window into the body. So in 1872 he entered Yale's Sheffield Scientific School. Six months later, he began medical school at the College of Physicians and Surgeons in New York City. It was a typical good American medical school—it had absolutely no requirements for admission and no grades in any course.

Welch graduated, and on April 19, 1876, he sailed for Europe to continue his scientific education. He was going to Germany, where the best science was then being done. He was hardly alone in seeking more knowledge there. One historian has estimated that between 1870 and 1914, fifteen thousand American doctors studied in Germany or Austria, along with thousands more from England, France, Japan, Turkey, Italy, and Russia.

Welch expected to have to practice medicine to make a living, and he recognized how helpful to such a career studying in Germany could be. He assured his sister and brother-in-law as well as his father, all of whom were helping support him financially, "The prestige and knowledge which I should acquire by a year's study in Germany would decidedly increase my chance of success. The young doctors who are doing well in New York are in a large majority those who have studied abroad."[1]

But his real interest lay with the tiny minority of Americans who went to Germany to explore a new universe: he wanted to learn laboratory science. In America he had already acquired a reputation for knowing far more than his colleagues. But in Germany he was refused acceptance into two laboratories because he knew so little. This inspired rather than depressed him. Soon Welch found a place to start and excitedly wrote home,

I feel as if I were only just initiated into the great science of medicine. My previous experiences compared with the present are like the difference between reading of a fair country and seeing it with one's own eyes. To live in the atmosphere of these scientific workshops and laboratories, to come into contact with the men who have formed and are forming the

science of today, to have the opportunity of doing a little
original investigation myself are all advantages, which, if
they do not prove fruitful in later life, will always be to me a
source of pleasure and profit.[2]

By 1878 Welch was back in New York and looking for work. At no time in history had medicine been advancing so rapidly. The thousands who flocked to Europe were proof of American physicians' intense interest in those advances. Yet in the United States neither Welch nor anyone else could support themselves by either joining in that great march or teaching what they had learned.

So Welch began teaching a laboratory course. There were no microscopes, no glassware, no incubators, no instruments. Facing the empty rooms, discouraged, he wrote, "I cannot make much of a success out of the affair at present. I seem to be thrown entirely upon my own resources for equipping the laboratory and do not think that I can accomplish much."[3]

He was also worried. His entire compensation would come from student fees, and the three-month course was not required. Would he earn enough money to live on? He confided to his sister, "I sometimes feel rather blue when I look ahead and see that I am not going to be able to realize my aspirations in life . . . There is no opportunity in this country, and it seems unlikely there ever will be . . ."[4]

He was wrong.

Welch's course quickly became extraordinarily popular. Soon students from all three of New York City's medical schools were lining up for it, attracted as Welch had been to this new science, to the microscope, to experimentation.

But despite the throngs of motivated students taking his course, Welch did not prosper. Two years went by, then three, then four. To cobble together a living, he did autopsies at a state hospital, served as an assistant to a prominent physician, and tutored medical students before their final exams. But as he passed his thirtieth birthday he was doing no real science. Little medical research was being done in America at the time. Yet in Europe science was marching from advancement to advancement, breakthrough to breakthrough.

In 1884 Welch finally received a job offer from the Hopkins. At the Hopkins—which became known simply as "Hopkins," as it's called today—Welch would be expected to create an institution that would alter American medicine forever. When he accepted the position, he was thirty-four years old.

✛

The greatest challenge of science lies in asking an important question and framing it in a way that allows it to be broken into manageable pieces, into experiments that can be conducted to ultimately lead to answers. To do this requires a certain kind of genius, one that allows someone to weave together seemingly unconnected bits of information. It allows an investigator to see what others do not see, to make leaps of connectivity and creativity. This, in turn, can lead an investigator deeper and deeper into something, which creates new information.

The best investigators ask the question "So what?" Like a word on a Scrabble board, this question can connect with and prompt movement in many directions. It can eliminate a piece of information as unimportant or, at least to the investigator asking the question, irrelevant. To consider questions like this requires *wonder*, a deep wonder focused by discipline.

William Welch had a vital and wide curiosity, but he did not have this deeper wonder. He could not see the large in the small. Instead, he examined a problem, then moved on. Welch's failing as a researcher was this: In science, as in the rest of his life, he lived upon the surface. His attention never settled upon one important or profound question. The research he did was first-rate. But in the context of an entire lifetime, it did not amount to much.

Instead, Welch's real genius lay in two areas. First, he had not only knowledge but judgment. He had an extraordinary ability to hear someone describe their experiments, or read a paper, and immediately define the series of experiments needed to clarify the crucial points. He had an equally extraordinary ability to judge people, to identify those with the promise to do what he had not done. Second, Welch inspired. He inspired unconsciously, simply by being himself. He seemed so comfortable with himself that he gave comfort to those around him. He exuded confidence without arrogance.

American medical education needed a revolution. When the Hopkins medical school opened in 1893, most American medical schools had still not established any affiliation with either a teaching hospital or a university; most faculty salaries were still paid by student fees (meaning that anyone who could pay their way was accepted into medical school); no other medical school required a college degree, much less any knowledge of biology, physics, or chemistry; and students still often graduated without ever touching a patient. By contrast, the Hopkins paid faculty salaries itself, and it required medical students to have not only a college degree with a background in science courses but also fluency in French and German so they could read foreign scientific articles. The school's requirements were so rigorous that Welch worried no students would enroll.

But students did come. Motivated and self-selected, they flocked to a school where students did not simply listen to lectures and take notes. They trooped through hospital rooms, examined patients, and made diagnoses. They performed autopsies and conducted laboratory experiments, and they explored: they explored organs with scalpels, nerves and muscles with electric currents, the invisible with microscopes.

By the first decade of the twentieth century, Welch had become the glue that cemented together the entire American medical establishment. He became a national figure, first within the profession, then within science, then in the larger world, serving as president or chairman of nineteen different major scientific organizations, including the American Medical Association and the National Academy of Sciences. One colleague said that Welch had "the power to transform men's lives almost by the flick of a wrist."[5]

He used his power to transform American medical education both directly and indirectly. His recommendation meant everything. Stanford University president Ray Wilbur neither flattered nor overstated when he wrote Welch, "Not to turn to you for information in regard to the best men to fill vacancies in our medical school would be to violate all the best precedents of American medical education."[6]

One area Welch focused on was finishing the reform of all medical education. The example of the Hopkins had forced more and faster changes at the best universities—such schools as Harvard, Columbia, the University of Pennsylvania, and the University of Michigan—and their leaders joined Welch in his quest to improve medical education. So did the American Medical Association.

But most medical schools were almost unaffected by the Hopkins example. That remained the case until Welch protégé Abraham Flexner, who would later bring Albert Einstein to the Institute for Advanced Study at Princeton University, wrote a report titled *Medical Education in the United States and Canada*. It soon came to be known simply as the Flexner Report.

Flexner dismissed many medical schools as "without redeeming features of any kind . . . general squalor . . . clinical poverty . . . One encounters surgery taught without patient, instrument, model, or drawing; recitations in obstetrics without a [mannequin] in sight—often without one in the building."[7]

According to his investigation, few—very, very few—schools met any reasonable standard. Flexner recommended that more than 120 of the 150-plus American medical schools in operation be closed. The report made the front page of newspapers. Remarkably, nearly one hundred medical schools did close or merge within a few years. Those that survived improved dramatically.

In addition to his influence on medical education, Welch played another, hugely important role: directing the flow of tens of millions of dollars into laboratory research.

✚

On January 2, 1901, John D. Rockefeller Sr.'s grandchild died of scarlet fever in Chicago. Later that year, the Rockefeller Institute for Medical Research was incorporated in New York City. This was no coincidence, and it would change everything.

Welch declined an offer to head the new institute, but he assumed all the duties for launching it, chairing both the institute's board itself and its board of scientific directors. At first the institute gave modest grants to scientists elsewhere, but in 1903 it opened its own laboratory. In 1910 a small affiliated hospital to investigate disease was added to the institute; the physician Rufus Cole served as its first director.

Cole was tall, mustached, and elegant; he did not appear to be a forceful man. But his thinking was powerful. Cole urged the directors of the institute "that the hospital laboratory be developed as a true research laboratory."[8] Cole was setting an enormously important precedent. He was calling for—demanding—that physicians treating patients undertake rigorous research involving patients with disease. This kind of work had been seen elsewhere, but not in the systematic way Cole envisioned.

Such studies not only threatened the power of scientists doing purely laboratory research at the institute but also changed the doctor-patient relationship. They were an admission that doctors did not know all the answers and could not learn them without the patients' help.

The Rockefeller Institute Hospital opened in 1910, following Cole's vision of applying science directly to patient care. This created *the* model of clinical research—a model followed today by the greatest medical research facility in the world, the Clinical Center at the National Institutes of Health in Bethesda, Maryland. That model allowed investigators to learn. It also prepared them to act.

In less than thirty years, thanks to some healthy competition and significant financial investment, institutions like the Hopkins and the Rockefeller Institute revolutionized American medicine from an old-fashioned and disorganized practice to a modernized and science-based discipline and gave it a true claim to scientific leadership.

✛

Welch had turned the Hopkins model into a force. And on the eve of America's entry into World War I, he had one more goal. Back in 1884, when the Hopkins first offered Welch his position, he had urged the establishment of a separate school to study public health in a scientific manner. Public health, the branch of medicine that deals primarily with hygiene and disease prevention, was and is where the largest numbers of lives are saved. Understanding a disease's epidemiology—its patterns, where and how it emerges and spreads—allows that disease to be prevented or contained. Epidemiology can help prevent an epidemic, or the widespread occurrence of an infectious disease. Science had first contained epidemic diseases including smallpox, then cholera, then typhoid, then plague, then yellow fever through large-scale public health measures. Everything from filtering water, to testing, to killing rats, to vaccination was used to avoid widespread outbreak of disease. Public health measures lack the drama of pulling someone back from the edge of death, but they save lives by the millions.

Only one school of public health existed in the United States, at Tulane University in New Orleans, established in 1916. Welch had put aside his goal of opening another such school while he focused on transforming American medicine. Now he began to pursue that goal again.

The Johns Hopkins School of Hygiene and Public Health, with Welch serving as its first dean, opened on October 1, 1918. The study of epidemic disease was, of course, a prime focus of the public health school.

It turned out that Welch was sick the day of the scheduled opening, and getting sicker. He had recently wrapped up a trip to investigate a strange and deadly epidemic. His symptoms were identical to those of the victims of that epidemic. He would soon realize that he, too, had the disease that would become known as influenza.

CHAPTER THREE

❧

A Mutant Swarm

To understand what happened in 1918—and also in 2020—one must first understand viruses and the concept of the mutant swarm.

Viruses are themselves a mystery that exist on the edges of life. They are not simply small bacteria. Bacteria consist of only one cell, but they are fully alive. Each has a metabolism, requires food, produces waste, and reproduces by division. Most bacteria cause no harm to people. But some do; infections including strep throat and tuberculosis are bacterial.

Viruses, on the other hand, do not eat or burn oxygen for energy. They do not engage in any process that could be considered metabolic. They do not produce waste. They do not reproduce. They make no side products, by accident or design. They are less than a fully living organism but more than an inert collection of chemicals. Antibiotics, which first appeared in the late 1930s and 1940s, usually kill bacteria. At first they seemed to perform like magic, and by the 1960s public health officials were declaring victory over infectious disease. But antibiotics have no effect whatsoever on viruses.

The differences between viruses and bacteria wouldn't be established until 1926. It was Thomas Rivers, a Hopkins-trained scientist, who defined the differences between them. Rivers went on to create the field of virology, the study of viruses, and become one of the world's leading virologists and head of the Rockefeller Institute Hospital.

Several theories of viruses' origins exist, and evidence exists to support all of them. And different viruses may have developed in different ways. Whatever its origin, a virus has only one function: to replicate itself. But unlike other life forms (if a virus is considered a life form), a virus does not even do that itself. It invades cells that have energy, and then, like some alien puppet master, it takes them over, forces them to make thousands, and in some cases hundreds of thousands, of new viruses. The power to do this lies in its genes.

Genes resemble software; just as a sequence of computer code tells the computer what to do—whether to run a word processing program, a computer game, or an internet search—genes tell the cell what to do. In most life forms, genes are stretched out along the length of a strand-like molecule of DNA. But many viruses—including influenza, SARS-CoV-2, and HIV—encode their genes in RNA, ribonucleic acid, an even simpler but less stable molecule.

Computer code is a binary language: it has only two numbers, zero and one. The genetic code uses a language of four letters, each representing chemicals. DNA and RNA are strings of these chemicals. In effect they are very long sequences of letters. Sometimes these letters do not form words or sentences that make any known sense: 97 percent of human DNA contains no genes; its function is still unknown.

But when the letters spell out words and sentences that *do* make sense, then that sequence is, by definition, a gene.

When a gene in a cell is activated, it orders the cell to make particular proteins. Proteins can be used like bricks, as building blocks of tissue. (The proteins that one eats, like seafood, meat, and eggs, generally do end up building tissue.) But proteins also play crucial roles in most chemical reactions within the body, as well as in carrying messages to start and stop different processes. Insulin, for example, is a hormone but also a protein; it helps regulate metabolism, and it particularly affects blood glucose levels.

When a virus successfully invades a cell, it inserts its own genes into the cell and seizes control. The cell's internal machinery then begins producing what the viral genes demand instead of what the cell needs for itself.

So the cell turns out hundreds of thousands of viral proteins, which bind together with copies of the viral genome to form new viruses. Then the new viruses escape. In this process the host cell almost always dies, usually when the new viral particles burst through the cell surface to invade other cells.

Within the body, cells, proteins, viruses, and everything else constantly bump against one another and make physical contact. When they don't fit together, each moves on. Nothing happens.

But when one complements the other, if they fit together well enough, they "bind." Sometimes they fit loosely, in which case they may separate; sometimes they fit more snugly. Sometimes they fit with exquisite precision, like a specialized key for a highly secure lock.

When binding occurs, events unfold. Things change. The body reacts.

There are three different types of influenza viruses: A, B, and C. Type C rarely causes disease in humans. Type B does cause disease, but not epidemics. Only influenza A viruses cause epidemics or pandemics—an epidemic being a local or national outbreak; a pandemic, a worldwide one, including the pandemic of 1918.

Influenza viruses did not originate in humans. Their natural home is in wild aquatic birds, and many more variants of influenza viruses exist in birds than in humans. Massive exposure to an avian virus can infect humans directly, but an avian virus cannot pass easily from person to person. Unless, that is, it first changes; unless it first adapts to humans.

This happens rarely, but it does happen. The virus may also go through another mammal to get to humans; swine are an especially effective intermediary mammal for viruses that jump to humans. Whenever a new variant of the influenza virus does adapt to humans, it will threaten to spread rapidly across the world. It will threaten a pandemic.

When an organism reproduces, its genes try to make exact copies of themselves. But sometimes mistakes—also called mutations—occur in this process.

This is true whether the genes belong to people, plants, or viruses. The more advanced the organism, however, the more mechanisms exist to prevent mutations. A person mutates at a much slower rate than bacteria, bacteria mutate at a much slower rate than a virus, and a DNA virus mutates at a much slower rate than an RNA virus.

DNA is double-stranded, and one strand has to match the other strand, which provides a kind of automatic proofreading mechanism to cut down on copying mistakes. Most RNA viruses are single-stranded and have no proofreading mechanism whatsoever, no way to protect against mutation. So viruses that use RNA to carry their genetic information mutate much faster still.

Different RNA viruses mutate at different rates as well. A few mutate so rapidly that virologists don't even consider them to be a population of copies of the same virus—instead, they are called a mutant swarm.

These mutant swarms contain trillions and trillions of closely related but different viruses. Even the viruses produced from a single cell will include many different versions of themselves.

Most of these mutations interfere with the functioning of the virus and will either destroy the virus outright or destroy its ability to infect. But other mutations, sometimes in a single letter in its genetic code, will allow the virus to adapt rapidly to a new situation.

Influenza is an RNA virus. So are HIV and the coronavirus. And, of all RNA viruses, influenza and HIV are among those that mutate the fastest. The influenza virus mutates so fast that

99 percent of the new viruses that burst out of a cell in the reproduction process are too defective to infect another cell and reproduce again. But that still leaves 1 percent of viruses, or between one thousand and ten thousand, that *can* infect another cell.

Both influenza and HIV fit the concept of a mutant swarm. And the influenza virus reproduces rapidly—far faster than HIV. Therefore it adapts rapidly as well, often too rapidly for the immune system to respond.

Influenza and other viruses—not bacteria—combine to cause approximately 90 percent of all respiratory infections, including sore throats. But influenza is not simply a bad cold. It is a quite specific disease, with a distinct set of symptoms and epidemiological behavior. In humans the virus normally attacks only the respiratory system, and it becomes increasingly dangerous as it penetrates deeper into the lungs. Indirectly it affects many parts of the body, and even a mild infection can cause pain in muscles and joints and intense headaches. It may also lead to far more grave complications.

The overwhelming majority of influenza victims—the disease also used to be referred to as "the grippe," from the French "la grippe"—usually recover fully within ten days. Partly because of this, and partly because the disease is confused with the common cold, influenza is rarely viewed with concern.

Yet even when outbreaks are not deadly as a whole, influenza strikes so many people that even the mildest viruses almost always kill. Currently in the United States, even without an epidemic or pandemic, the Centers for Disease Control and Prevention (CDC) estimate that influenza kills between three thousand and fifty-six thousand Americans a year, depending chiefly on the virulence, or strength, of that year's virus; how effective that year's vaccine is—because the virus mutates, it has to be redesigned every year—and how many people get vaccinated.

It is, however, not only an endemic disease, a disease that is always around. Influenza can arrive in epidemic form, spreading widely in a specific community. Or, when an influenza virus that has been infecting birds, pigs, or another animal jumps species and begins infecting humans when no human immune system has seen it before, it can spread in pandemic form, moving across continents and spreading worldwide. And pandemics can be more lethal—sometimes much, much more lethal—than endemic diseases.

Throughout known history there have been periodic pandemics of influenza, usually several a century. They erupt when a new influenza virus emerges. And the nature of the influenza virus makes it inevitable that new viruses emerge.

PART II

---+---

THE US ARMY AND INFLUENZA

CHAPTER FOUR

❦

America Goes to War

In the spring of 1918, death was no stranger to the world. More than five million soldiers had already died in World War I, and all of Europe was weary of the war. Only in the United States were some people, most of them concentrated on the East Coast and many of them holding positions of power or influence, not weary. Only in the United States did some still regard war as glorious. And nearly a year earlier those people had put intense pressure on President Woodrow Wilson to enter the conflict.

On April 2, 1917, after his cabinet unanimously called for war, Wilson delivered his war message to Congress.

Two days later, Wilson explained to a friend, "It was necessary for me by very slow stages and with the most genuine purpose to avoid war to lead the country on to a single way of thinking." Wilson had wanted the United States to enter the war with a sense of selfless mission, believing glory possible, while still keeping itself separate from the rest of the world. The United States fought alongside Britain, France, Italy, and Russia.

Anyone who believed that Wilson's reluctant embrace of war meant that he would not pursue it aggressively knew nothing of him. "To fight you must be brutal and ruthless," he said, "and the spirit of ruthless brutality will enter into the very fibre of our national life, infecting Congress, the courts, the policeman on the beat, the man in the street."[1]

Wilson declared, "It isn't an army we must shape and train for war; it is a nation."[2] To train the nation, Wilson used an iron fist minus any velvet glove. He did have some legitimate reasons to justify a hard line.

For reasons entirely unrelated to the war, America was a rumbling chaos of change and movement, its very nature and identity shifting. In 1870 the United States' population was only forty million, 72 percent of whom lived in small towns or on farms. By the time America entered the war, the population had increased to roughly 105 million. Between 1900 and 1915 alone, fifteen million immigrants flooded the United States; most came from eastern and southern Europe, with new languages and religions, along with darker complexions. And the first census after the war would also be the first one to find more people living in urban areas than rural.

Wilson's hard line was designed to intimidate those reluctant to support the war into doing so and to crush or eliminate those who would not. The single largest ethnic group in the United States was German American, and a large German-language press had been sympathetic to Germany. Would German Americans fight against Germany? Another large ethnic group had come from

Ireland, which was then entirely ruled by Britain; in 1916 the Irish rebelled and began fighting for an independent Ireland. Would Irish Americans fight on the side of Britain? The American Midwest was isolationist. Would it send soldiers across an ocean when the United States had not been attacked?

Prior to US entry in the war, Major Douglas MacArthur had written a long proposal advocating for outright censorship if the nation did join the struggle. Journalist Arthur Bullard, who was close to Wilson's confidant "Colonel" Edward House, argued for another approach. Congress's rejection of censorship settled the argument in Bullard's favor.

Bullard had written from Europe about the war for magazines including *Outlook*, *Century*, and *Harper's Weekly*. He pointed out that Britain was censoring the press and had misled the British people, undermining trust in the government and support for the war. He had no particular affection for truth per se, only for effectiveness. "Truth and falsehood are arbitrary terms," he wrote. "There is nothing in experience to tell us that one is always preferable to the other . . . There are lifeless truths and vital lies . . . The force of an idea lies in its inspirational value. It matters very little if it is true or false."[3]

Wilson aide Walter Lippmann wrote the president a memo encouraging him to create a publicity bureau on April 12, 1917, a week after America declared war. The day after receiving the memo, Wilson issued Executive Order 2594, creating the Committee on Public Information (CPI), and he named George Creel, a journalist and prominent Wilson supporter, its head.

Creel was passionate, intense, handsome, and wild. He intended to create "one white-hot mass . . . with fraternity, devotion, courage, and deathless determination."[4]

Creel did this through tens of thousands of press releases and feature stories that were routinely run unedited by newspapers. And those same publications instituted a self-censorship. They would print nothing that might hurt morale. Creel also created a force of "Four Minute Men"—their number ultimately exceeded one hundred thousand—who gave brief speeches to increase public support of the war before the starts of meetings, movies, and entertainment of all kinds.

Creel began intending to report only facts, if carefully selected ones, and conducting only a positive campaign, avoiding the use of fear as a tool. But this soon changed. The new attitude was embodied in a declaration by one of Creel's writers that "inscribed in our banner even above the legend Truth is the noblest of all mottoes—'We Serve.'"[5] They served a cause. One poster designed to sell Liberty Bonds warned, "I am Public Opinion. All men fear me! . . . If you have the money to buy and do not buy, I will make this No Man's Land for you!"[6] Another CPI poster targeted German loyalists, declaring, "You find him in hotel lobbies, smoking compartments, clubs, offices, even homes . . . He is a scandal-monger of the most dangerous type. He repeats all the rumors, criticism, and lies he hears about our country's part in the war. He's very plausible . . . People like that . . . through their vanity or curiosity or *treason*, they are helping German propagandists sow the seeds of discontent . . . If you find a disloyal person in your search, give his name to the Department of Justice in Washington and tell them where to find him."

Creel demanded "100 percent Americanism" and planned for "every printed bullet [to] reach its mark."[7] Simultaneously, he told the Four Minute Men that fear was "an important element to be bred in the civilian population. It is difficult to unite a people by talking only on the highest ethical plain. To fight for an ideal, perhaps, must be coupled with thoughts of self-preservation."[8]

Music that might hurt morale was prohibited. Military camps banned such songs as "I Wonder Who's Kissing Her Now," along with "questionable jokes and other jokes, which while apparently harmless, have a hidden sting—which leave the poison of discontent and worry and anxiety in the minds of the soldiers and cause them to fret about home."[9]

Finally, upon urging from Wilson, Congress passed an updated Sedition Act, which made it punishable by twenty years in jail to "utter, print, write or publish any disloyal, profane, scurrilous, or abusive language about the government of the United States." One could go to jail for cursing the government or criticizing it even if what one said was true. Oliver Wendell Holmes wrote the Supreme Court opinion ruling the law constitutional, arguing that the First Amendment did not protect speech if "the words used . . . create a clear and present danger."

✚

Wilson's hard-line approach informed nearly everything that happened in the country, including fashion: to save cloth, a war material—everything was a war material—designers narrowed lapels and shrank or eliminated pockets.

States outlawed the teaching of German, while an Iowa politician warned that "ninety percent of all the men and women who teach the German language are traitors."[10] Conversations in German on the street or over the telephone became suspicious. Sauerkraut was renamed "liberty cabbage."

Thousands of government posters and advertisements urged people to report to the Justice Department anyone "who spreads pessimistic stories, divulges—or seeks—confidential military information, cries for peace, or belittles our effort to win the war."[11]

The federal government also took control over much of national life. The War Industries Board allocated raw materials to factories, guaranteed profits, and controlled production and prices of war materials. The Railroad Administration essentially controlled the American railroad industry. The Fuel Administration controlled fuel distribution, and to save fuel it also instituted daylight saving time. The Food Administration controlled agricultural production, pricing, and distribution. And the government inserted itself into the minds of Americans by allowing only its own voice to be heard, by both threatening objectors with prison and shouting down everyone else.

In addition to his hard line, Wilson also tried to lead the nation down a softer path. And that approach meant the American Red Cross.

The International Committee of the Red Cross had been founded in 1863 to protect and assist victims of conflict, with a focus on war and on the decent treatment of prisoners as set forth in the first Geneva Convention. In 1881 Clara Barton had founded the American Red Cross, and the next year the United States accepted the guidelines of the Geneva Convention, which require humane treatment for anyone taken into enemy hands. All of the countries fighting in World War I were members of the International Committee of the Red Cross. But each national unit was fully independent.

The American Red Cross was a partially public institution whose president, at least officially, was (and still is) the president of the United States. Officially chartered by Congress to serve the nation in times of emergency, the American Red Cross grew even closer to the government during the war.

As soon as the United States entered World War I, the American Red Cross declared that it would "exert itself in any way which . . . might aid our allies . . . The organization seeks in this great world emergency to do nothing more and nothing less than to coordinate the generosity and the effort of our people toward achieving a supreme aim."[12]

There was no more patriotic organization. It had full responsibility for supplying nurses, tens of thousands of them, to the military. It organized fifty base hospitals in France. It equipped several railroad cars as specialized laboratories in case of disease outbreaks—but reserved them for use only by the military, not by civilians—and stationed them "so that one may be delivered at any point [in the country] within twenty-four hours."[13] (The Rockefeller Institute also outfitted railroad cars as state-of-the-art laboratories and placed them around the country.) It cared for civilians injured or made homeless after several explosions in munitions factories.

But its most important role had nothing to do with medicine or disasters. Its most important function was to bind the nation together, and Wilson used it to reach into every community in the country. The Red Cross did not waste the opportunity to increase its presence in American life. The American Red Cross began the Great War with only 107 local chapters. It finished with 3,864 chapters, stretching from the largest cities and into the smallest villages.

In 1918 the Red Cross counted thirty million Americans—out of a total population of 105 million—as active supporters. Eight million Americans, nearly 8 percent of the entire population, served as production workers in local chapters. Women made up nearly all this enormous volunteer workforce, and they might as well have worked in factories. Each chapter received a quota, and each chapter produced that quota. They made millions of sweaters, millions of blankets, millions of socks. They made furniture. They did everything requested of them, and they did it well. When the federal Food Administration said that pits from peaches, prunes, dates, plums, apricots, olives, and cherries were needed to make carbon for gas masks, newspapers reported, "Confectioners and restaurants in various cities have begun to serve nuts and fruit at cost in order to turn in the pits and shells, a patriotic service . . . Every American man, woman, or child who has a relative or friend in the army should consider it a matter of personal obligation to provide enough carbon-making material for his gas mask."[14] And so Red Cross chapters throughout the country collected thousands of tons of fruit pits—so many that they were told, finally, to stop.

✚

The full engagement of the nation had begun the instant Wilson had chosen war. Initially the American Expeditionary Forces in Europe was small. But the American army was massing. That process would jam millions of young men into extraordinarily tight quarters in barracks built for far fewer. It would bring millions of workers into factories and cities where there was no housing, where men and women not only shared rooms but beds, where they not only shared beds but shared beds in shifts, where one shift of workers came home—if their room could be called a home—and climbed into a bed just vacated by others leaving to go to work, where they breathed the same air, drank from the same cups, used the same knives and forks.

Technology has always mattered in war, but this was the first truly scientific war, the first war that matched engineers and their abilities to build not just artillery but submarines and airplanes and tanks, the first war that matched laboratories of chemists and physiologists devising or trying to counteract the most lethal poison gas.

The person who had the chief responsibility for the performance of military medicine was surgeon general of the army William Crawford Gorgas. The army gave him little authority with which to work, but Gorgas was able to accomplish much in the face of even outright opposition from those above him. Gorgas, along with Welch, was part of the leadership of key national medical committees. They committed themselves to ensuring that the best medical science be available to the military. Welch, now sixty-seven years old, three decades older than when he'd taken charge of the Hopkins, short, obese, and out of breath, put a uniform on, devoted much time to army business, and took a desk in Gorgas's personal office that he used whenever in Washington, DC. From the beginning of their planning, these leaders focused on the biggest killer in war—not combat, but epidemic disease.

In wars throughout history, more soldiers had died of disease than in battle or of their wounds. And epidemic disease had routinely spread from armies to civilian populations.

This was true not just in ancient times or in the American Civil War, in which two men died from disease for every battle-related death. More soldiers had died of disease than combat even in the wars fought since scientists had adopted modern public health measures. In the Boer War that raged from 1899 to 1902 between Britain and the white settlers of South Africa, ten British troops died of disease for each combat-related death.

✛

When the war began, there were 140,000 physicians in the United States. Only 776 of them were serving in the army or navy. The military needed tens of thousands of physicians, and it needed them immediately. Most would have volunteered even if they were not drafted. Most wanted to participate in this great crusade. The entire Rockefeller Institute was incorporated into the army. Men in uniforms marched down laboratory and hospital corridors. Nearly all research shifted to something war-related, or to instruction.

Nursing had, like medicine, changed radically in the late nineteenth century. It, too, had become scientific. But changes in nursing involved factors that went beyond the purely scientific; they involved status, power, and the role of women. Nursing was one of the few fields that gave women opportunity. And it was a field they controlled. While Welch and his colleagues were revolutionizing American medicine, Jane Delano, Lavinia Dock, and others were doing the same to nursing. They did so with little support from physicians, all of whom were male and many of whom felt threatened by intelligent and educated nurses. In some hospitals, physicians replaced labels on drug bottles with numbers so nurses could not question a prescription.

In 1912, before becoming surgeon general, Gorgas had anticipated that if war ever came, the army would need vast numbers of nurses, many more than would likely be available. He believed, however, that not all of them would have to be fully trained. He wanted to create a corps of "practical nurses" who lacked the education and training of "graduate nurses."

Others were also advancing this idea, but they were all men.

The women who ran nursing would have none of it. Jane Delano, proud and intelligent as well as tough, driven, and authoritarian, had just left the army to establish the Red Cross nursing program, and the Red Cross had all the responsibility for supplying nurses to the army, evaluating, recruiting, and often assigning them.

Delano rejected Gorgas's practical nurses plan, telling her colleagues it "seriously threatened" the status of professional nursing. She told the Red Cross bluntly that "if this plan were put through I should at once sever my connection with the Red Cross . . . [and] every member of the state and local committee would go out with me."[15]

The Red Cross and the army surrendered to her. When the United States entered the war, it had 98,162 graduate nurses, women whose training probably exceeded that of many—if not most—doctors trained before 1910. The war sucked up nurses as it sucked up everything else. In May 1918 roughly sixteen thousand nurses were serving in the military. Gorgas believed that the army alone needed fifty thousand.

The triumph of the nursing profession over the Red Cross and the United States Army, an army at war, was extraordinary. That the victors were women made it more extraordinary.

In the meantime, the military's appetite for doctors and nurses only grew. Four million American men were under arms with more coming, and Gorgas was planning for three hundred thousand hospital beds. The number of trained medical staff he had simply could not handle that load. So the military suctioned more and more nurses and physicians into its camps, aboard ships, into

France, until it had extracted nearly all the best young physicians. And so medical care for civilians deteriorated rapidly. The doctors who remained in civilian life were largely either incompetent young ones or those over forty-five years of age, the vast majority of whom had been trained in the old ways of medicine. The shortage of nurses would prove even more serious. Indeed, it would prove deadly.

CHAPTER FIVE

⚜

Keeping the Troops Healthy

The US Army had exploded from tens of thousands of soldiers before the war to millions in a few months. Huge cantonments, temporary quarters each holding roughly fifty thousand men, were thrown together in a matter of weeks. Hundreds of thousands of men occupied them before the camps were completed. They were jammed into those barracks that were finished, barracks designed for far fewer than their number, while tens of thousands of young soldiers lived through the first winter in tents. Hospitals were the last buildings to be constructed.

These circumstances not only brought huge numbers of men into intimate proximity but also mixed farm boys and city boys from hundreds of miles away, each of them with entirely different disease immunities and vulnerabilities. Never before in American history—and possibly never before in any country's history—had so many men been brought together in such a way. Even at the front in Europe, even with the importation there of labor from China, India, and Africa, the concentration and throwing together of men with different vulnerabilities may not have been as explosive a mix as that in American training camps.

As surgeon general of the army, Gorgas's nightmare was of an epidemic sweeping through those camps. Given the way troops moved around from camp to camp, if an outbreak of infectious disease erupted in one, it would be extraordinarily difficult to isolate that camp and keep the disease from spreading to others. Thousands, possibly tens of thousands, could die. Such an epidemic might spread to the civilian population as well. Gorgas intended to do all within his power to prevent his nightmare from becoming real.

By 1917 medical science was far from helpless in the face of disease. It had achieved considerable success in manipulating the immune system and in public health. Vaccines prevented a dozen diseases that devastated livestock. Investigators had also gone far beyond the first success against smallpox and were now developing vaccines to prevent a host of diseases as well as antitoxins and serums to cure them. Science had triumphed over diphtheria. Sanitary and public health measures were containing typhoid, cholera, yellow fever, and bubonic plague, and vaccines against typhoid, cholera, and plague also appeared. Treatments for snake bites and dysentery were found. A tetanus shot brought magical results—in 1903, before its widespread use in the United States, 102 people died out of every one thousand treated for tetanus; ten years later, universal use of the treatment lowered the death rate to zero per one thousand treated. The possibilities of manipulating the immune system to defeat infectious disease seemed to hold enormous promise.

At the management level, Gorgas was taking action, too. He saw to it that many of the new army doctors assigned to the cantonments were trained at the Rockefeller Institute. He began stockpiling huge quantities of vaccines, antitoxins, and sera (the plural of "serum"), all of which had been produced by people he could rely on. He transformed several railroad cars into the most modern laboratory facilities, paid for not by the government but by the Rockefeller Institute.

Also, even before construction began on the cantonments, Gorgas created a special unit for "the prevention of infectious disease."[1] He assigned the very best to it. Welch headed this unit, which included five other members of international renown. They laid out precise procedures for the army to follow to minimize the chances of an epidemic.

Meanwhile, as troops were pouring into camps, Rockefeller Institute colleagues Rufus Cole and Oswald Avery, and others who had turned their focus to pneumonia, issued a specific warning: "Although pneumonia occurs chiefly in endemic form, small and even large epidemics are not unknown . . . Pneumonia [seems] especially likely to attack raw recruits."[2]

Gorgas's army superiors ignored the advice. As a result, the army soon suffered a taste of epidemic disease. It would be a test run, for both a virus and medicine.

✚

The winter of 1917–18 was the coldest on record east of the Rocky Mountains. Barracks were jam-packed, and hundreds of thousands of men were still living in tents. Camp hospitals and other medical facilities had not yet been finished. An army report conceded the failure to provide warm clothing or even heat. But most dangerous was the overcrowding.

In that bitterly cold winter, measles came to the army's barracks, and it came in epidemic form. Usually measles infects children and causes only fever, rash, cough, runny nose, and discomfort. But like many other children's diseases—especially viral diseases—when measles strikes adults, it often strikes hard. Early in the twenty-first century, measles is still causing one million deaths a year worldwide.

As infected soldiers moved from camp to camp, measles moved with them, rolling through camps like a bowling ball knocking down pins.

The army issued orders forbidding men from crowding around stoves, and officers entered barracks and tents to enforce it. But, especially for the tens of thousands who lived in tents in the record cold, it was impossible to keep men from crowding around the one source of warmth.

Of all the complications of measles, the most deadly by far was pneumonia. The average death rate from it in twenty-nine cantonments was twelve times that of civilian men of the same age. Pneumonia was the leading cause of death around the world, greater than tuberculosis, greater than cancer, greater than heart disease, greater than plague.

And, like measles, when influenza kills, it usually kills through pneumonia.

Pneumonia maintained its position as the leading cause of death in the United States until 1936. It and influenza are so closely linked that modern international health statistics, including those compiled by the CDC, routinely classify them as a single cause of death. Even now, early in the twenty-first century, with antibiotics, antiviral drugs, oxygen, and intensive-care units, influenza and pneumonia combined routinely rank as the fifth or sixth leading cause of death in the United States and the leading cause of death from infectious disease. It varies year to year, usually depending on the severity of the influenza season. COVID-19 replaced influenza in 2020; at this writing it's unknown whether it will maintain its place as the leading killer among infectious diseases or whether a combination of improved vaccines, treatments, and immune response will cause it to fall back behind influenza.

✛

Oswald Avery was a short, thin, fragile man who weighed at most 110 pounds. Born in Montreal, he grew up in New York City. He seemed friendly, cheerful, even outgoing, but he had very little personal life. He almost never invited over friends and rarely went out to dinner. Although he was close to and felt responsible for his younger brother and an orphaned cousin, his life, his world, was his research.

Avery arrived at the Rockefeller Institute in 1913 when he was already forty years old. By that age, many of his contemporaries had already made names for themselves. Yet Avery had made no particular mark as an investigator—but not from lack of ambition, nor from lack of work.

For years he shared an apartment with Alphonse Dochez, another scientist at Rockefeller. In the laboratory they focused on the pneumococcus—a bacterium that is the single most common cause of pneumonia. They worked in simple spaces with simple equipment. Each room had a single deep porcelain sink and several worktables, each with a gas outlet for a Bunsen burner and drawers underneath. The tabletop space was filled with racks of test tubes, mason jars, petri dishes, droppers for various dyes and chemicals, and tin cans holding pipettes and platinum loops. On the same tabletop investigators performed nearly all their work: inoculating, bleeding, and dissecting animals. Also on the tabletop was a cage for the occasional animal kept as a pet.

First they replicated earlier experiments that others had performed, partly to familiarize themselves with techniques. They exposed rabbits and mice to gradually increasing dosages of pneumococci. Soon the animals' immune systems responded by developing antibodies to the bacteria. (Antibodies are a part of the body's defense system and work to destroy disease-causing bacteria.) They created a serum from those antibodies and succeeded in curing mice with the serum. Others had done that, too. But the mice were not people.

No one anywhere had made any progress in curing people. Experiment after experiment had failed. Elsewhere other investigators trying similar approaches quit, convinced by their failures that their theories were wrong or that their techniques were not good enough to yield results—or they simply grew impatient and moved on to easier problems.

Avery did not move on. He saw snatches of evidence suggesting he was right. He persisted, experimenting repeatedly, trying to learn from each failure. His background in both chemistry and immunology began paying off. Avery's understanding of the bacteria deepened. It deepened enough that he forced scientists to change their thinking about the immune system.

With the rest of the Western world already at war, Cole, Avery, Dochez, and their colleagues were ready to test their immune serum in people.

✚

Even when Cole first tried the new serum on patients it showed promise. He and Avery immediately devoted themselves to refining their procedures in the laboratory. Then they began a careful series of trials with a finished product. They found that giving large dosages of serum—half a liter via IV—cut the death rate of Type I pneumonias by more than half, from 23 percent to 10 percent.

It was not a cure. Pneumonias caused by other types of pneumococci did not yield so easily. But of all pneumonias, those caused by Type I pneumococci were the single most common. Cutting the death rate by more than half in the single most common pneumonia was progress, real progress.

In October 1917, Gorgas told army hospital commanders that "in view of the probability that pneumonia will be one of the most important diseases amongst the troops,"[3] they must send even more doctors to the Rockefeller Institute to learn how to prepare and administer this serum.

Simultaneously Cole, Avery, and Dochez were developing a vaccine to prevent pneumonia caused by Type I, II, and III pneumococci. After proving it worked in animals, they and six other Rockefeller researchers turned themselves into guinea pigs, testing its safety in humans by giving each other massive doses. All of them had negative reactions to the vaccine itself; three had severe reactions. They decided that the vaccine was too dangerous to administer in those dosages but planned another experiment with lower doses administered once a week for four weeks, which gave recipients time to gradually build up immunity.

Cole and his organization were ready for a large test in March 1918. The vaccine was given to twelve thousand troops at Camp Upton on Long Island, New York. That used up all the vaccine available. Another nineteen thousand troops served as controls, receiving no vaccine. Over the next three months, not a single vaccinated soldier developed pneumonia caused by any of the types of pneumococci vaccinated against. The controls suffered 101 cases. This result was not absolutely conclusive. But it strongly suggested that the vaccine worked. And it was a far better result than was being achieved anywhere else in the world.

If Avery and Cole could develop a serum or vaccine with

real effectiveness against pneumonia, it would be the greatest triumph medical science had yet known.

Both the prospect of finally being able to defeat pneumonia and its appearance in the army camps only intensified Gorgas's determination to find a way to limit its killing. He asked Welch to create a special pneumonia board supported by all the knowledge and resources of Gorgas and Welch and the institutions they represented. Cole would serve as its chair. Avery would lead the actual laboratory investigations and stay in New York. Most of the others would work in the field.

On a regular basis, Cole traveled to Washington, DC, to discuss the latest findings with Welch and senior army medical officers in Gorgas's office. Cole, Welch, and others had also been conducting rigorous inspections of cantonments, checking on everything from the quality of the camp's surgeons, bacteriologists, and epidemiologists right down to the way camp kitchens washed dishes. Any recommendations they made were immediately ordered to be carried out.

On June 4, 1918, Cole, Welch, and several other members of the pneumonia board appeared in Gorgas's office once more. This time the discussion was wide-ranging, focusing on how to minimize the possibility of something worse than the measles epidemic. They were all worried about Gorgas's epidemic nightmare.

They were not particularly worried about influenza, although they were tracking outbreaks of the disease. For the moment those outbreaks were mild, not nearly as dangerous as the measles epidemic had been. They well knew that when influenza kills, it kills through pneumonia, but they felt prepared. Gorgas had already asked the Rockefeller Institute to gear up its production and study of the pneumonia serum and vaccine, and both the institute and the Army Medical School had launched major efforts to do so.

Then the conversation turned from the laboratory to epidemiological issues. The inspection tours of the camps had convinced members of the board that cross infection between people in the camps had caused many of the measles-related pneumonia deaths. To prevent such a problem from happening again, Cole suggested creating contagious-disease wards with specially trained staffs, something the best civilian hospitals had. They also discussed overcrowding in hospitals and isolation of troops. Welch advised establishing "detention camps for new recruits where men are kept for ten to fourteen days."[4]

They all recognized the difficulty of convincing the army to do this, and of convincing the army to end the even more serious problem of overcrowding in barracks.

Still, another army medical officer injected one piece of good news. He said that the problem of overcrowding in the hospitals themselves had been eliminated. Every army hospital had at least one hundred empty beds as of May 15, for a total of twenty-three thousand beds empty. Every single epidemiological statistic the army collected showed improved overall health. He insisted that facilities and training were adequate.

Time would tell.

CHAPTER SIX

❦

Unusual Outbreak

It is not known where the influenza pandemic of 1918 began. There are theories of origin that include Vietnam, China, and a British Army post in France. But Frank Macfarlane Burnet, a Nobel laureate who lived through the pandemic and spent most of his scientific career studying influenza, later concluded that the evidence was "strongly suggestive" that the 1918 influenza pandemic began in the United States and that its spread was "intimately related to war conditions and especially the arrival of American troops in France." Numerous other scientists agree with him.

The first recognized cases occurred in Kansas, and the first recognized large-scale outbreak occurred at Camp Funston, the second-largest military camp in the country, which held on average fifty-six thousand young troops. It was built at the intersection of the Smoky Hill and Republican Rivers, where they form the Kansas River. It was located on Fort Riley, one of the largest military installations in the United States. Like all the other training camps in the country, Funston had been thrown together in literally a few weeks in 1917. There the army prepared young men for war.

It was a typical camp, with typical tensions between army regulars and men who had until recently been civilians. There were also the usual clashes of egos, especially since Camp Funston and Fort Riley had different commanding officers.

Funston was typical in another way. The winter of 1917–18 was one of record cold, and, as the army itself conceded, at Funston as elsewhere "barracks and tents were overcrowded and inadequately heated, and it was impossible to supply the men with sufficient warm clothing."

So army regulations—written for health reasons—detailing how much space each man should have were violated, and men were stacked in bunks with insufficient clothing and bedding and inadequate heating. That forced them to huddle ever more closely together around stoves to try to keep warm.

On March 4, a private at Funston, a cook, reported to the camp hospital ill with influenza. Within three weeks, more than eleven hundred Funston soldiers were sick enough to be admitted to the hospital, and thousands more—the precise number was not recorded—needed treatment at infirmaries scattered around the base. Pneumonia developed in 237 men, roughly 20 percent of those hospitalized, but only thirty-eight men died. While that was a higher death toll than one would normally expect from influenza, it was not so high as to draw attention.

All influenza viruses mutate constantly, spinning off variants. Whoever carried the virus to Funston brought a mild version of it, but it was a version capable of becoming lethal.

A constant river of soldiers moved between Funston, other army bases, and France. In total, twenty-four of the thirty-six largest army camps experienced an influenza outbreak that spring. Thirty of the fifty largest cities in the country, most of them adjacent to military facilities, also suffered an April spike in "excess mortality" from influenza, although that did not become clear except in hindsight. At first it seemed like nothing to worry about. The only thing at all worrisome was that the disease was moving.

The first unusual outbreaks of influenza activity in Europe occurred in Brest, France, where American troops disembarked, in early April 1918. And from Brest the disease spread, and quickly. Still, although many got sick, these outbreaks were generally mild. Troops were temporarily debilitated, then recovered.

The first appearance of influenza in the French army came on April 10. Then it struck Paris in late April, and at about the same time the disease reached Italy. In the British army the first cases occurred in mid-April; then the disease exploded. A British army report noted, "At the end of May it appeared with great violence . . . The numbers affected were very great . . . A brigade of artillery had one-third of its strength taken ill within forty-eight hours."[1] In June troops returning from mainland Europe introduced the disease into England.

But again the complications were few, and nearly all the troops recovered. The only serious concern—and it was serious indeed—was that the disease would undermine the troops' ability to fight.

That seemed the case in the German army. German troops in the field suffered sharp outbreaks beginning in late April.

In the meantime, it was in Spain that the virus picked up its name. Spain actually had few cases before May 1918, but the country was neutral during the war, which meant that the government did not censor the press. Spanish papers were filled with reports of the disease, especially when Spain's King Alfonso XIII fell seriously ill. This reporting stood in stark contrast to French, German, and British newspapers, which printed nothing negative, nothing that might hurt morale.

The disease soon became known as "Spanish influenza" or "Spanish flu," very likely because only Spanish newspapers were publishing accounts of the spread of the disease that were picked up in other countries.

It struck Portugal, then Greece. The earliest cases in Bombay (now known as Mumbai) erupted at the end of May. Influenza also reached Shanghai, China, around the same time. Said one observer, "It swept over the whole country like a tidal wave."[2] In June and July, death rates across England, Scotland, and Wales surged. Also in June, Germany suffered initial sporadic outbreaks, and then a full-fledged epidemic swept across all the country.

Denmark and Norway began suffering in July; Holland and Sweden, in August. It jumped to New Zealand and then Australia in September; in Sydney it sickened 30 percent of the population.

But though it was spreading explosively, it continued to appear not to be a violent disease. Of 613 American troops admitted to the hospital during one outbreak in France, only one man died.

In the French army, fewer than one hundred deaths resulted from forty thousand hospital admissions.

In fact, its mildness made some physicians wonder whether this disease actually was influenza. Three British doctors wrote a journal article that concluded that the epidemic could not actually be influenza because the symptoms, though similar to those of influenza, were too mild, "of very short duration and so far absent of relapses or complications."[3]

That article was dated July 13, 1918.

+

When the virus began jumping from army camp to army camp and occasionally spreading to adjacent cities in the United States in March and April, leaders of the Rockefeller Institute showed little concern about it, and neither did Avery commence any laboratory investigation.

But as influenza surged across Europe they began to pay attention. In France in late May—not even two months after the first outbreak in the French army—at one small station of 1,018 French army recruits, 688 men were ill enough to be hospitalized, and forty-nine died. When 5 percent of an entire population—especially of healthy young adults—dies in a few weeks, that is frightening.

Between June 1 and August 1, more than two hundred thousand out of two million British soldiers in France were hit hard enough that they could not report for duty even in the midst of desperate combat. By mid-June, Welch, Cole, Gorgas, and others were trying to gather as much information as possible about the progression of influenza in Europe.

But then the disease was gone. On August 10, the British command declared the epidemic over at the front. In Britain itself, on August 20, a medical journal stated that the influenza epidemic "has completely disappeared."[4]

In the United States, influenza had neither swept through the country nor completely died out. Perhaps the most loaded word in science is "interesting." Influenza was about to become interesting. For the virus had not disappeared. It had only gone underground, like a forest fire that burns in the roots of trees, preparing to explode in flame once again. It was mutating, adapting, watching, and waiting.

CHAPTER SEVEN

❦

Lethal Waves

Like other influenza pandemics—at least eleven have occurred in the last three hundred years—and COVID-19, the 1918 influenza pandemic came in waves. The first spring wave killed few, but the second wave would be lethal. Three hypotheses could explain this phenomenon.

One is that the mild and deadly diseases were caused by two entirely different viruses. This is highly unlikely. Many victims of the first wave demonstrated significant protection from the second wave; in fact, illness in the first wave protected against illness or death in the second wave better than any modern influenza vaccine, which provides strong evidence that the deadly virus was a variant of the mild one.

The second possibility is that a mild virus caused the spring epidemic and that in Europe it encountered a second influenza virus. The two viruses infected the same cells, "reassorted" their genes, and created a new and lethal virus. But at least some scientific evidence directly contradicts this hypothesis, and most influenza experts today do not believe this happened.

The third explanation involves the adaptation of the virus to people.

When the 1918 virus jumped from animals to people and began to spread, it would have suffered a shock of its own as it adapted to a new species. At first, it was not perfect in its ability to infect humans. As a later study would conclude, the first wave "had a tendency to peter out . . . It lacked the penetrating power of the second wave." The virus had to adjust, to mutate, to create variants that became better and better at infecting humans. Evolutionary pressure drove this natural process to improve, even to perfect, the virus's ability to transmit between people, but evolution did not put any pressure on the virus to become more virulent, more lethal, more deadly. In 1918, however, as the virus improved its ability to transmit between humans, as it became better and better at infecting its new host, it did turn lethal. It had already shown this potential—as when it killed forty-nine soldiers, 5 percent of the entire camp, in just a few weeks. That potential was about to be fulfilled.

✚

On June 30, 1918, the British freighter *City of Exeter* docked at Philadelphia after a brief hold at a maritime quarantine station. The ship was laced with deadly disease, but Rupert Blue, the civilian surgeon general and head of the US Public Health Service, had issued no instructions to the maritime service to hold influenza-ridden ships. So it was released.

Nonetheless, the condition of the crew was so frightening that a British official had arranged in advance for the ship to be met at a wharf empty of anything except ambulances whose drivers wore surgical masks. Dozens of crew members "in a desperate condition" were taken immediately to Pennsylvania Hospital, where, as a precaution against infectious disease, a ward was sealed off for them. One after another, crew members died.

They seemed to die of pneumonia, but it was a pneumonia accompanied by strange symptoms, including bleeding from the nose. A report noted, "The opinion was reached that they had influenza."[1]

In 1918 all infectious disease was frightening. Americans had already learned that "Spanish influenza" was serious enough that it had slowed the German offensive. Rumors now unsettled Philadelphia that these deaths, too, came from Spanish influenza. But those in control of the war's propaganda machine still wanted nothing printed that could hurt morale. Two physicians stated flatly to newspapers that the men had not died of influenza. They were lying.

The disease did not spread. The brief quarantine had held the ship long enough that the crew members were no longer contagious when the ship docked. This particular virus, finding no fresh fuel, had burned itself out. The city had dodged a bullet.

By now the virus had undergone numerous passages through humans. Even while medical journals were commenting on the mild nature of the disease, all over the world hints of a vicious outbreak were appearing.

Earlier some physicians had insisted that the disease was not influenza because it was too mild. Now others also began to doubt that this disease was influenza—but this time because it seemed too deadly.

Many histories of the pandemic portray the eruption of deadly disease—the hammer blow of the second wave—as sudden and simultaneous in widely separated parts of the world, and therefore deeply puzzling. But it is not so puzzling. Likely, as happened with COVID-19, variants with similar properties emerged at about the same time in different locations. And this lethal variant of the virus was finding its home in humans. On three continents separated by thousands of miles of ocean, the killing was about to begin.

✚

Nearly 40 percent of the two million American troops who arrived in France—791,000 men—disembarked at Brest, a deepwater port capable of handling dozens of ships simultaneously. Troops from all over the world came through there. Like many other cities, Brest had seen a burst of influenza in the spring, although it had been mild.

The first outbreak with high mortality in Brest occurred in July, in a detachment of American troops from Camp Pike, Arkansas. They occupied an isolated camp, and the outbreak initially seemed contained. It was not. By August 10, the same day the British army declared the influenza epidemic over, so many

French sailors stationed at Brest were hospitalized with influenza and pneumonia that they overwhelmed the naval hospital there and forced it to close. And the death rate among them began soaring.

American troops continued pouring into and then out of Brest, mixing with French troops also training in the vicinity. When soldiers of both armies left the vicinity, they dispersed the virus en masse.

Meanwhile, on August 15 the HMS *Mantua* arrived in Freetown, Sierra Leone, a major coaling center on the West African coast that serviced ships traveling from Europe to South Africa and Asia. The *Mantua* arrived with two hundred crew members suffering from influenza. When local laborers who had been exposed to the ship's crew returned to their homes, they carried more than their wages. Soon influenza spread through the force of men who coaled the ships. And this influenza was not mild. On August 24, two local residents died of pneumonia while many others were still sick.

On August 27, the HMS *Africa* pulled into port in Freetown. This ship, too, needed coal, but five hundred of the six hundred laborers of the Sierra Leone Coaling Company did not report to work that day. The crew helped load the coal, working side by side with African laborers. The *Africa* carried a crew of 779. Within a few weeks, nearly six hundred were sick. And 51 were dead— 7 percent of the entire crew.

The transport HMS *Chepstow Castle*, carrying troops from New Zealand to the front, stopped for coal at Freetown on August 26 and 27; within three weeks, influenza struck down nine hundred of her 1,150 men. The death toll was 38.

Officials soon after estimated that influenza killed 3 percent of the entire African population in Sierra Leone itself, nearly all of them dying within the next few weeks. More recent evidence suggests that the death toll was most likely considerably more than that, possibly double that figure—or higher.

✚

Across the Atlantic, at Commonwealth Pier in Boston, the navy operated what they called a "receiving ship." It was actually a barracks where as many as seven thousand sailors in transit ate and slept in what the navy itself called "grossly overcrowded"[2] quarters.

On August 27, two sailors reported to sick bay with influenza. On August 28, eight more sailors reported ill. On August 29, fifty-eight men were admitted.

As in Brest and Freetown and aboard ship, men began to die. Any hopes of containing the disease had collapsed. On September 3, a civilian suffering from influenza was admitted to the Boston City Hospital. On September 4 students at the Naval Radio School at Harvard University, in Cambridge across the Charles River from Boston proper, fell ill.

And then came Devens.

✚

Camp Devens sat on five thousand acres in rolling hills thirty-five miles northwest of Boston. It included fine farmland along the Nashua River. In August 1917 it opened with fifteen thousand men although the camp was incomplete—its sewage was still being discharged directly into the Nashua River rather than being safely treated and processed.

Like most other camps, it had suffered from measles and pneumonia outbreaks. But the medical staff was first-rate. An inspection of the Devens hospital had given it an excellent review down to its kitchen; the report noted, "The mess officer is well informed and alert."[3]

The main problem at Devens was that it was built to hold a maximum of thirty-six thousand men. On September 6, Devens held just over forty-five thousand men. Still, the camp hospital could accommodate twelve hundred, and it was caring for only eighty-four patients. With enough medical personnel to run several simultaneous research efforts, with a highly competent clinical staff, with a virtually empty hospital, Devens seemed ready for any emergency.

It wasn't.

On September 7, a soldier from D Company, Forty-Second Infantry Division, was sent to the hospital. He ached to the extent that he screamed when he was touched, and he was delirious. He was diagnosed as having meningitis, an infection that causes inflammation around the brain and spinal cord.

The next day a dozen more men from his company were hospitalized and suspected of having meningitis. It was a reasonable diagnosis. Symptoms did not resemble those of influenza, and a few months earlier the camp had suffered a minor epidemic of meningitis.

Over the next few days, other Devens organizations began reporting cases of influenza-like disease. The medical staff, good as it was, did not at first connect these various cases to one another, nor to the outbreak on Commonwealth Pier. They made no attempt to quarantine cases. In the first few days no records of influenza cases were even kept because they "were looked upon as being examples of the epidemic disease which attacked so many of the camps during the spring"[4]—in other words, too mild to be worthy of comment. In the overcrowded barracks and mess halls, the men mixed. A day went by. Two days. Then, suddenly, noted an army report, "Stated briefly, the influenza . . . occurred as an explosion."[5]

It exploded indeed. In a single day, 1,543 Camp Devens soldiers reported ill with influenza. On September 22, 19.6 percent of the entire camp was on sick report, and almost 75 percent of those on sick report had been hospitalized. By then the pneumonias, and the deaths, had begun.

On September 24 alone, 342 men were diagnosed with pneumonia. Devens normally had 25 physicians. Now, as army and civilian medical staff poured into the camp, more than 250 physicians were treating patients. The doctors, the nurses, and the orderlies went to work at 5:30 a.m. and worked steadily until 9:30 p.m., slept, then went at it again. Yet on September 26 the medical staff was so overwhelmed, with doctors and nurses not only ill but dying, they decided to admit no more patients to the hospital, no matter how ill.

The Red Cross, itself by then overwhelmed by the spread of the disease to the civilian population, managed to find twelve more nurses and sent them in. They were of little help. Eight of the twelve collapsed with influenza; two died.

For this was no ordinary pneumonia. Roy Grist, one of the army physicians at the hospital, wrote a colleague, "These men start with what appears to be an ordinary attack of La Grippe or Influenza, and when brought to the Hosp. they very rapidly develop the most vicious type of pneumonia that has ever been seen. Two hours after admission they have the Mahogany spots over the cheek bones, and a few hours later you can begin to see the Cyanosis"—when people's features darken because their blood is not carrying oxygen—"extending from their ears and spreading all over the face, until it is hard to distinguish the coloured men from the white . . . It is only a matter of a few hours then until death comes . . . It is horrible. One can stand it to see one, two or twenty men die, but to see these poor devils dropping like flies . . . We have been averaging about 100 deaths per day . . . Pneumonia means in about all cases death . . . We have lost an outrageous number of Nurses and Drs . . . It takes special trains to carry away the dead. For several days there were no coffins and the bodies piled up something fierce . . . It beats any sight they ever had in France after a battle . . . Good By old Pal, God be with you till we meet again."[6]

✚

Welch, Cole, and others, all of them colonels now, had just finished a tour of southern army bases. It was not their first such tour, and as before, knowing that an army barracks offered explosive tinder, they had been inspecting camps to find and correct any practice that might allow an epidemic to gain a foothold. They also spent much time discussing pneumonia. After leaving Camp Macon in Georgia, they had retired for a few days of relaxation to Asheville, North Carolina, the most fashionable summer retreat in the South.

The group returned to Washington, DC, on a Sunday morning relaxed and in good spirits. But their mood changed abruptly as they stepped off the train. An escort had been waiting for them, and his anxiety quickly communicated itself. He was taking them to the surgeon general's office—immediately. Gorgas himself was in Europe. His deputy barely looked up as they opened the door: "You will proceed immediately to Devens. The Spanish influenza has struck that camp."[7]

They arrived at Devens eight hours later in a cold and drizzling rain. The entire camp was in chaos, the hospital itself a battlefield. The war had come home indeed. As they entered the hospital, they watched a continuous line of men filing in from the barracks carrying their blankets or being themselves carried.

Care was almost nonexistent. The base hospital, designed for twelve hundred, could accommodate at most twenty-five hundred. It now held in excess of six thousand. All beds had long since been filled. Every corridor, every spare room, every porch was filled, crammed with cots occupied by the sick and dying. There was nothing antiseptic or sterile about the sight. And there were no nurses. When Welch arrived, seventy out of two hundred nurses were already sick in bed themselves, with more falling ill each hour. He performed an autopsy himself and said, "This must be some new kind of infection or plague."[8]

Welch walked out of the autopsy room and made three phone calls: Boston, New York, and Washington, DC. In Boston he spoke to Burt Wolbach, a Harvard professor and chief pathologist at the great Boston hospital the Brigham. Welch asked Wolbach to perform many autopsies. Perhaps the dead could reveal a clue to this strange disease.

Welch also knew that any treatment or prevention for this would have to come from the laboratory. His second call was to New York, to the Rockefeller Institute, where he summoned Oswald Avery. Avery had been refused a commission in the Rockefeller army unit because he was Canadian, but on August 1 he had become an American citizen. By coincidence, the same day Welch called him, Avery was promoted from private to captain. More importantly, he had already begun investigating the pneumococcus.

Later that day both Avery and Wolbach arrived and immediately began their respective tasks.

The third call Welch made was to Washington, DC, to Charles Richard, the acting army surgeon general while Gorgas was in Europe at the front.

Richard responded instantly, sending orders to all medical personnel to isolate and quarantine all cases and segregate soldiers from civilians outside the camps: "It is important that the influenza be kept out of the camps, as far as practicable . . . Epidemics of the disease can often be prevented, but once established they cannot well be stopped."[9]

He also warned both the army adjutant general and chief of staff, "New men will almost surely contract the disease. In transferring men from Camp Devens a virulent form of the disease will almost surely be conveyed to other stations . . . During the epidemic new men should not be sent to Camp Devens, nor should men be sent away from that camp."

The next day, with reports already of outbreaks in other camps, Richard tried to impress upon the chief of staff the lethality of the disease. He urged that the transfer of personnel from one camp to another be all but eliminated except for the most "urgent military necessities."[10]

✚

On August 27, the same day the first sailors at Commonwealth Pier had fallen ill, the steamer *Harold Walker* had departed Boston, bound for New Orleans. En route fifteen crew members had fallen ill; in New Orleans the ship unloaded its cargo and put three crewmen ashore. The three men died. By then the *Harold Walker* had already proceeded to Mexico.

On September 4, physicians at the New Orleans naval hospital made the first diagnosis of influenza in any military personnel in the city; the sailor had arrived in New Orleans from the Northeast. That same date, a second patient also reported ill with influenza;

he was serving in New Orleans. Forty of the next forty-two patients who entered the hospital had influenza or pneumonia.

By then hundreds of sailors had already gone from Boston to naval bases around the country, including north of Chicago to the Great Lakes Naval Training Station, the largest facility of its kind in the world.

On September 8, at the Newport Naval Base in Rhode Island, more than one hundred sailors reported sick.

The virus was reaching south along the coast, jumping inland to the Midwest, spanning the nation to the Pacific.

All over the world, the virus was adapting to humans, achieving maximum efficiency. And, all over the world, the virus was turning lethal.

As the virus moved, two parallel struggles emerged. One encompassed all of the nation. Within each city, within each factory, within each family, into each store, onto each farm, along the length of the track of the railroads, along the rivers and roads, deep into the bowels of mines and high along the ridges of the mountains, the virus would find its way. In the next weeks, the virus would test society as a whole and each element within it. Society would have to gather itself to meet this test, or collapse.

The other struggle lay within one tight community of scientists. They—men like Welch, Avery, and Cole—had been drafted against their will into a race. They knew what was required. They knew the puzzle they needed to solve. They were not helpless. They had some tools with which to work. They knew the cost if they failed.

But they had very little time indeed.

PART III

FEAR

CHAPTER EIGHT

~✦~

A Model City

On September 7, 1918, three hundred sailors arrived from Boston at the Philadelphia Navy Yard. They would light a match in that city, and what happened in Philadelphia from that point would unfortunately prove to be a model for what would happen too often elsewhere.

Philadelphia was already typical in its war experiences. Every city was being flooded by people, and shipbuilding alone had added tens of thousands of workers. Overcrowded before the war, Philadelphia now literally teemed with people. In 1918 the city's slums were deemed by a national publication for social workers to be worse than the tenements on the Lower East Side of New York. African Americans endured even more squalid conditions, and Philadelphia had the largest African American population of any northern city, including New York and Chicago.

Housing was scarce, and two, three, or four entire families would cram themselves into a single two- or three-room apartment, with children and teenagers sharing a bed. In rooming houses laborers shared not just rooms but beds, often sleeping in shifts just as they worked in shifts.

The city offered the poor social services in the form of Philadelphia Hospital, a poorhouse, and an asylum. But it provided nothing else, not even an orphanage. The social elite and progressives ran whatever charitable activities that did exist. Even normal services such as schools were in short supply.

All this made Philadelphia fertile ground for epidemic disease.

Four days after the arrival of the sailors from Boston at the navy yard, nineteen sailors reported ill with symptoms of influenza.

Lieutenant Commander R. W. Plummer, a physician and chief health officer for the Philadelphia naval district, was well aware of the epidemic's rage. Determined to contain the outbreak, he ordered the immediate quarantine of the men's barracks and the meticulous disinfecting of everything the men had touched.

In fact, the virus had already escaped, and not only into the city. One day earlier, 334 sailors had left Philadelphia for Puget Sound in the Pacific Northwest; many would arrive there desperately ill.

Plummer also immediately called in Paul Lewis.

Lewis had been expecting such a call. He loved the laboratory more than he loved anyone or anything, and he had the full confidence of the leaders of the Rockefeller Institute, whom he had worked for as a young scientist. Now a leader of a different scientific institute at the University of Pennsylvania, he was focusing on lung disease, particularly tuberculosis.

No one needed to tell Lewis the urgency of the influenza situation. It was up to him to take charge of what would normally be the step-by-step, deliberate process of tracking down the pathogen, or agent that caused the disease, and trying to develop a serum or vaccine. And there was no time for normal scientific procedures.

The next day, eighty-seven sailors reported ill. By September 15, while Lewis and his assistants worked in labs at the University of Pennsylvania and at the navy hospital, the virus had made six hundred sailors and marines sick enough to require hospitalization, and more men were reporting ill every few minutes. The navy hospital ran out of beds and began sending ill sailors to a civilian hospital.

On September 17, five doctors and fourteen nurses in that civilian hospital suddenly collapsed. None had exhibited any prior symptoms whatsoever. One moment, they felt normal; the next, they were being carried in agony to hospital beds.

✚

The epidemic was sweeping through the Philadelphia naval installations with comparable violence, as it had in Boston. Yet in Philadelphia, despite the news out of Boston, despite events at its own navy yard, the city's public health director Wilmer Krusen had done absolutely nothing.

Krusen publicly denied that influenza posed any threat to the city. He made no contingency plans in case of emergency, stockpiled no supplies, and created no lists of medical personnel who would be available in an emergency, even though 26 percent of Philadelphia's doctors and an even higher percentage of its nurses were in the military.

Krusen insisted to reporters that the dead were not victims of an epidemic; he acknowledged that they had died of influenza but insisted it was only "old-fashioned influenza or grip." The day after he spoke, fourteen sailors died. So did the first civilian, "an unidentified Italian."

The following day, more than twenty victims of the virus went to a morgue. One was a nurse who had cared for the first sailors to come to the civilian hospital. She was twenty-three years old.

Krusen's public face remained nothing but reassuring. He now conceded that there were "a few cases in the civilian population" and said that health inspectors were looking for cases among civilians "to nip the epidemic in the bud," but he did not say how.

On September 28, a great Liberty Loan parade, designed to sell millions of dollars of war bonds, which would help pay for the war, was scheduled. Weeks of organizing had gone into the event. It was to be the greatest parade in Philadelphia history, with thousands marching in it and hundreds of thousands expected to watch it. Hundreds of thousands of people would be crowded together in the city's streets.

✛

These were unusual times. The Great War made them so. One cannot look at the influenza pandemic without understanding the context.

Already two million US troops were in France; it was expected that at least two million more would be needed. Every element of the nation, from farmers to elementary school teachers, was enlisted in the war—willingly or otherwise. To Wilson, to his entire administration, and to allies and enemies alike, the control of information mattered. Advertising was about to emerge as an industry; after the war it would claim the ability to "sway the ideas of whole populations."[1]

Total war requires sacrifice. The sacrifices included inconveniences in daily life. To contribute to the war effort, citizens across the country endured "meatless days" during the week and one "wheatless meal" every day. All these sacrifices were of course voluntary, completely voluntary—although the Food Administration could effectively close businesses that did not "voluntarily" cooperate. And if someone chose to go for a drive in the country on a "gasless Sunday," when people were "voluntarily" refraining from driving, that someone was pulled over by hostile police.

The Wilson administration intended to make the nation come together. The preservation of morale itself became an aim, because if morale faltered, all else might as well. And the preservation of morale meant free speech was threatened. The government had an organization with two hundred thousand members who spied on neighbors and coworkers. The organization advised citizens, "Call the bluff of anyone who says he has 'inside information.' Tell him that it's his patriotic duty to help you find the source of what he's saying. If you find a disloyal person in your search, give his name to the Department of Justice in Washington and tell them where to find him."[2]

The Liberty Loan campaign would raise millions of dollars in Philadelphia alone. The parade, critical to the campaign, was scheduled for September 28. Several doctors—practicing physicians, public health experts at medical schools, infectious disease experts—urged Krusen to cancel it.

Influenza was a disease spread in crowds. "Avoid crowds" was the advice Krusen and the Philadelphia Board of Health gave. To prevent crowding, the Philadelphia Rapid Transit Company had just limited the number of passengers in streetcars.

On September 27, the day before the parade, Philadelphia hospitals admitted two hundred more people—123 of them civilians—suffering from influenza. Krusen felt intense and increasing pressure to cancel the parade.

Krusen declared that it would proceed as planned.

None of the anxiety of the moment was reported in any of the city's five daily papers, and if any reporter questioned either Krusen or the Board of Health about the wisdom of the parade's proceeding, no mention of it appeared in print.

On September 28, marchers in the greatest parade in the city's history proudly stepped forward. The paraders stretched at least two miles—two miles of bands, flags, Boy Scouts, women's auxiliaries, marines, sailors, and soldiers. Several hundred thousand people jammed onto the parade route, crushing against one another to get a better look, the ranks behind shouting encouragement over shoulders and past faces to the brave young men. It was a grand sight indeed.

Krusen had assured them they were in no danger.

✚

The incubation period of influenza is twenty-four to seventy-two hours. Two days after the parade, Krusen issued a somber statement: "The epidemic is now present in the civilian population and is assuming the type found in naval stations and cantonments."

To understand the full meaning of that statement, one must understand precisely what was occurring in the army camps.

Boston's Camp Devens had been struck by surprise. The other cantonments and navy bases were not. Gorgas's office had issued immediate warnings of the disease, and medical staffs around the country took heed. Even so, the virus reached these military posts first. And with most lethality.

CHAPTER NINE

❧

Camp Grant

Illinois's Camp Grant sprawled across rolling country on the Rock River outside Rockford, Illinois. Most recruits there came from northern Illinois and Wisconsin, farm boys with straw-colored hair and flushed cheeks who knew how to raise the crops and produced them in plenty.

It was a remarkably orderly place, given the haste with which it had been built. It had neat rows of wooden barracks and more rows of large barrack tents, eighteen men to each. All the roads were dirt, and in late summer dust filled the air, except when rain turned the roads to mud. The hospital was situated at one end of the camp and had two thousand beds, although the most patients it had cared for at one time was 852; several infirmaries were also scattered throughout the base.

In June 1918, Welch, Cole, and others had inspected the camp and come away impressed. Welch judged Grant's chief medical officer, Lieutenant Colonel H. C. Michie, "capable and energetic," the hospital laboratory "excellent," and the pathologist "a good man," while Joe Capps, a friend of Cole's, was "of course an excellent chief of service"[1] at the hospital itself. The camp's veterinarian, who was responsible for several hundred horses and assorted livestock, had also impressed them favorably.

During that June visit they had all discussed pneumonia. Capps spoke of seeing a disturbing trend toward a "different type of pneumonia . . . clinically more toxic and fatal."[2]

Then he demonstrated for them an innovation he had experimented with: the wearing of gauze masks by patients with respiratory disease. Welch called the mask "a great thing . . . an important contribution in prevention of spray infections."[3] He encouraged Capps to write an article for the *Journal of the American Medical Association* (*JAMA*). Cole agreed: "This is a very important matter in connection with the prevention of pneumonia."[4]

Welch came away from that inspection, the last one of that tour, recommending two things. First, it confirmed in him his desire to have new arrivals at all camps assigned for three weeks to specially constructed detention camps; these men would eat, sleep, drill—and be quarantined—together to avoid any cross infections with men already in camp. Second, he wanted Capps's use of masks extended to all camps.

Capps did write the *JAMA* article. He reported finding the masks so successful that after less than three weeks of experimenting he had abandoned testing and simply started using them as "a routine measure."[5] He also made the more general point that "one of the most vital measures in checking contagion" is eliminating crowding. "Increasing the space between beds in barracks, placing the head of one soldier opposite the feet of his neighbor, stretching tent flags between beds, and suspending a curtain down the center of the mess table, are all of proved value."

To prevent a few arriving individuals from infecting an entire camp, he also repeated Welch's recommendation to isolate transferred troops. Camp Grant had such a "depot brigade," a separate quarantine barracks for new recruits and transfers. Its stairways were built on the outside so guards could enforce the quarantine. But officers did not stay in the depot brigade; only enlisted men did.

Capps's article appeared in the August 10, 1918, issue of *JAMA*.

On August 8, Colonel Charles Hagadorn took command of Camp Grant. A short, brooding officer and a West Point graduate, unmarried at fifty-one years of age, he had devoted his life to the army and his soldiers. He had prepared for war all his life, studying it constantly and learning from experience as well as reading and analysis. Sometimes Hagadorn gave what seemed to be impulsive and even inexplicable orders, but they had a curve of reason behind them. He was determined to teach his soldiers to survive and to kill. Not to die. He cared about his troops and liked being surrounded by them.

One problem that confronted him seemed to have little to do with war. Camp Grant was over capacity. Only thirty thousand troops had been present when Welch had visited in June. Now they were in excess of forty thousand with no expectation of any decrease. Many men were forced into tents even though winter—

winter in northern Illinois, one year after a record cold—was only a few weeks away.

Army regulations defined how much space each soldier had in the barracks. These regulations had little to do with comfort and much to do with public health. In mid-September, Hagadorn decided to ignore the army regulations on overcrowding and move even more men from tents into barracks. Already the nights were cold, and they would be more comfortable there.

But by then Gorgas's office had issued warnings about the epidemic, and influenza had reached the Great Lakes Naval Training Station one hundred miles away. At Camp Grant, doctors watched for the first case. They even had an idea where it might occur. Dozens of officers had just arrived from Devens.

Hagadorn made a few concessions. On September 20 he issued several orders to protect the camp's health. To prevent the rise of dust, all roads would be oiled. And out of concern for influenza he essentially agreed to a quarantine: "Until further notice from these Headquarters, passes and permission to be absent from Camp . . . will not be granted to Officers or enlisted men, except from this office, and then only for the most urgent reasons."[6]

But he issued one more order that day as well: "There must as a military necessity be a crowding of troops. The Camp Surgeon under the circumstances authorizes a crowding in barracks . . . beyond the authorized capacity . . . This will be carried out at once as buildings are newly occupied."[7]

On September 21, the day after Hagadorn issued his order,

several men in the Infantry Central Officers Training School—the organization with officers from Devens—reported ill. They were immediately isolated in the base hospital.

It did little good. By midnight, 108 men from the infantry school and the unit next to it were admitted to the hospital. There each patient had a gauze mask placed over his mouth and nose.

All public gatherings were canceled, and the men were ordered not "to mingle in any manner with men of other organizations at any time . . . No visitors will be permitted in the area involved . . . Any barracks from which several cases are reported will be quarantined; its occupants will not be permitted to mingle in any way with the occupants of other barracks in the same organization."[8]

Guards enforced the orders strictly. But people infected with influenza can infect others before they feel any symptoms. It was already too late. Within forty-eight hours, every organization in the camp was affected.

The next day, hospital admissions rose to 194; the next, 371; the next, 492. Four days after the first officer reported sick, the first soldier died. In six days, the hospital went from 610 occupied beds to 4,102 occupied, almost five times more patients than it had ever cared for.

All training for war, for killing, ceased. Now men fought to stop the killing. Healthy soldiers were consumed with attending to the sick; 320 men were sent to the hospital as general support staff, then 260 more were added. Another 250 men did nothing but stuff sacks with straw to make mattresses. Several hundred others unloaded a stream of railroad cars full of medical supplies.

Hundreds more helped transport the sick or cleaned laundry—washing sheets, making masks—or prepared food.

Meanwhile, barely in advance of a threatening thunderstorm, one hundred carpenters worked to enclose thirty-nine verandas with roofing paper to keep the rain off the hundreds of patients exposed to the elements. The gauze masks Capps was so proud of, the masks Welch had praised, were no longer being made; Capps ran out of material and personnel to make them.

The medical staff itself was collapsing from overwork—and disease. Five days into the epidemic, five physicians, thirty-five nurses, and fifty orderlies were sick. Those numbers would grow, and the medical staff would have its own death toll.

Seven days into the epidemic, soldiers still capable of work converted nine more barracks into hospitals. There were shortages of aspirin, disinfectant, paper bags, disposable cups, and thermometers—and the thermometers that *were* available were being broken by men in delirium.

Forty more nurses arrived for the emergency, giving the hospital 383. It needed still more. All visitors to the base and especially to the hospital had already been prohibited "except under extraordinary circumstances."[9] Those "extraordinary circumstances" typically meant a soldier was ill enough that his family received official notice from the camp via telegram; 438 such telegrams had been handled the day before.

That number was still climbing, and rapidly. To deal with what soon became thousands of telegrams and phone calls each day, the Red Cross erected a large tent, floored, heated, and wired for electricity, with its own telephone system and rows of chairs. It resembled an auditorium where relatives waited to see desperately ill soldiers. More personnel were needed to escort these visitors to the sick. Still more personnel and more laundry facilities were needed just to wash the gowns and masks that every visitor donned.

And there was something else, something still worse.

✚

The same day that the first Camp Grant soldier died, 3,108 troops boarded a train leaving there for Camp Hancock outside Augusta, Georgia. The men leaving Grant on that train were jammed into the cars with little room to move about, layered and stacked as tightly as if on a submarine.

When the train arrived, 950 miles from where it had begun, more than seven hundred men—nearly one-quarter of all the troops on board—were taken directly to Camp Hancock's base hospital, quickly followed by hundreds more; in total, two thousand of the 3,108 troops would be hospitalized with influenza.

Hagadorn had become all but irrelevant to the running of Camp Grant. Now he yielded on every point to the medical personnel, did everything they asked, made every resource available to them. Yet nothing seemed even to slow the disease.

At some other army camps, even more soldiers would collapse almost simultaneously; indeed, at Camp Custer outside Battle Creek, Michigan, twenty-eight hundred troops reported ill—in a *single* day.

Before the epidemic, Capps had begun testing a pneumonia serum prepared from chickens. Capps had planned a series of "very carefully controlled"[10] experiments. But now, with nothing else to try, he administered the serum to all as it arrived—it was in short supply. It seemed to work: 234 men suffering from pneumonia received the serum, and only 16.7 percent of them died. Meanwhile, more than half of those who did not receive the serum died. But there simply wasn't enough of it.

Desperate efforts were being made to protect troops from the disease, or at least prevent complications. Despite these measures, the death toll kept rising.

On October 8, Lieutenant Michie reported the latest death toll to Colonel Hagadorn in his headquarters office. The colonel heard the report and nodded. When Michie left, Hagadorn told him to close the door behind him.

Death was all about him. In the papers on his desk, in the reports he heard, literally in the air he breathed. That evening, Hagadorn took his own life. He was fifty-one years old.

✚

Two days after Philadelphia's Liberty Loan parade, Wilmer Krusen issued that somber statement, that the epidemic in the civilian population "was assuming the type found in naval stations and cantonments."

Influenza was indeed exploding in the city. Within seventy-two hours after the parade, every single bed in each of the city's thirty-one hospitals was filled. And people began dying. Hospitals started refusing to accept patients—with nurses turning down hundred-dollar bribes—without a doctor's or a police order. Yet people lined up to get in. One woman remembered her neighbors going "to the closest hospital, the Pennsylvania Hospital at 5th and Lombard, but when they got there there were lines and no doctors available and no medicine available. So they went home, those that were strong enough."[11]

Medical care was making little difference anyway.

On October 1, the third day after the parade, the epidemic killed 117 in a single day. Soon the daily death toll from influenza alone would exceed the city's average *weekly* death toll from all other causes—all illnesses, all accidents, all criminal acts combined.

On October 3, only five days after Krusen had let the parade proceed, he banned all public meetings in the city—including, finally, further Liberty loan gatherings—and closed all churches, schools, and theaters. Even public funerals were prohibited.

In ten days—*ten days!*—the epidemic had exploded from a few hundred civilian cases and one or two deaths a day to hundreds of thousands ill and hundreds of deaths each day.

Federal, municipal, and state courts closed. Giant signs everywhere warned the public to avoid crowds and use handkerchiefs when sneezing or coughing. Other placards read "Spitting equals death." People who spat on the street were arrested—sixty in a single day. The newspapers reported the arrests—even while continuing to minimize the epidemic.

Physicians were themselves dying, three one day, two another, four the next. The newspapers reported those deaths—on inside pages with other obituaries—but still did not emphasize the epidemic. Health and city workers wore masks constantly.

What should I do? people wondered with dread. *How long will it go on?* Each day, people discovered that friends and neighbors who had been perfectly healthy a week—or a day—earlier were dead, while city authorities and newspapers continued to minimize the danger. The *Public Ledger* newspaper claimed nonsensically that Krusen's order banning all public gatherings was not "a public health measure" and reiterated, "There is no cause for panic or alarm."

On October 5, doctors reported that 254 people died that day from the epidemic, and the papers quoted public health authorities as saying, "The peak of the influenza epidemic has been reached." When 289 Philadelphians died the next day, the papers said, "Believing that the peak of the epidemic has passed, health officials are confident."

In each of the next two days, more than three hundred people died, and again Krusen announced, "These deaths mark the high-water mark in the fatalities, and it is fair to assume that from this time until the epidemic is crushed the death rate will constantly be lowered."

The next day, 428 people died, and the daily death toll would keep climbing for many days yet—approaching double even that figure.

Krusen said, "Don't get frightened or panic stricken over exaggerated reports."[12] But his reassurances no longer reassured.

It was a common practice in 1918 for people to hang a piece of crepe fabric on the door to mark a death in the house. There was crepe everywhere. "People were dying like flies," one man said. "On Spring Garden Street, looked like every other house had crepe over the door. People was dead there."[13]

But the most terrifying aspect of the epidemic was the piling up of bodies. Undertakers, themselves sick, were overwhelmed. They had no place to put bodies. Gravediggers either were sick or refused to bury influenza victims.

Then undertakers ran short of coffins. The few coffins available suddenly became unaffordable. There were soon no caskets left to steal.

Plague. In the streets people had been whispering the word. The word slipped, somehow, once, by accident, into a newspaper. The country's "morale" issue, the self-censorship, the intent by editors to put every piece of news in the most positive possible context, all meant that no newspaper used that word again. But how many trusted the newspapers anymore?

✝

On September 4, influenza had reached New Orleans. On September 7, it had reached the Great Lakes Naval Training Station. In the next few days, ports and naval facilities on the Atlantic and Gulf Coasts—in Newport, New London, Norfolk, Mobile, and Biloxi—also reported this new influenza.

The virus had spanned the country, establishing itself on the Atlantic, in the Gulf, on the Pacific, on the Great Lakes. It had not immediately erupted in epidemic form, but it had seeded itself. Then the seeds began to sprout.

The virus followed railroads and rivers into the interior of the continent, from New Orleans up the Mississippi River into the body of the nation, from Seattle to the East, from the Great Lakes training station to Chicago, and from there along the railroad lines in many directions.

On September 28, when the Liberty Loan paraders marched through the Philadelphia streets, there were as yet only seven cases reported in Los Angeles, two in San Francisco. But the virus would get there soon enough.

In Philadelphia, meanwhile, fear came and stayed. Death could come from anyone, anytime. People moved away from others on the sidewalk, avoided conversation; if they did speak, they turned their faces away to avoid the other person's breathing. People became isolated, increasing the fear.

The impossibility of getting help compounded the isolation. Eight hundred fifty Philadelphia doctors and more nurses were away in the military, while more than that number were sick. Philadelphia General Hospital was down to 126 nurses.

Philadelphia had five medical schools. Each one dismissed its classes, and third- and fourth-year students manned emergency hospitals being set up in schools and empty buildings all over the city. The Philadelphia College of Pharmacy closed as well, sending its students out to help druggists.

Nothing they were doing worked.

Literally hundreds of thousands of people in Philadelphia were falling ill. Virtually all of them, along with their friends and relatives, were terrified that, no matter how mild the symptoms seemed at first, within them moved an alien force, a seething, spreading infection, a live thing with a will that was taking over their bodies—and could be killing them. And those who moved about them were terrified, too—both for the victims and for themselves.

CHAPTER TEN

❦

Only Influenza

I t was influenza, only influenza.

This new influenza virus, like most new influenza viruses, spread rapidly and widely. The virus sickened tens of millions of people in the United States. In many cities more than half of all families had at least one victim ill with influenza; in San Antonio the virus made more than half the entire population ill. And it sickened hundreds of millions across the world.

But this was influenza, only influenza. The overwhelming majority of victims got well. They endured, sometimes a mild attack and sometimes a severe one, and they recovered.

The virus passed through this vast majority in the same way influenza viruses usually did. Victims had an extremely unpleasant several days (the unpleasantness multiplied by terror that they would develop serious complications) and then recovered within ten days. The course of the disease in these millions actually convinced the medical profession that this was indeed only influenza.

But in a minority of cases the virus manifested itself in an influenza that did not follow normal patterns, that was unlike any influenza ever reported.

Generally in the Western world, the virus demonstrated extreme virulence, or strength, leading to pneumonia in 10 to 20 percent of all cases. In the United States, this translated into two to three million cases of pneumonia. These numbers most likely translate into several hundred million severe cases around the world, in a world with a population less than one-third that of today.

This was still influenza, only influenza. The most common symptoms then, as now, are well known. Victims suffer headaches, body aches, fever, complete exhaustion, coughing. One clinician reported, "In nonfatal cases . . . the temperature ranged from 100 to 103 [degrees] F[ahrenheit]. Nonfatal cases usually recovered after an illness of about a week."[1]

Then there were the cases in which the virus struck with violence.

To those who suffered a violent attack, there was often pain—terrific pain—and the pain could come almost anywhere. Victims arrived with an extraordinary array of symptoms, symptoms either previously unknown entirely in influenza or experienced with previously unknown intensity. Initially, physicians—good physicians, intelligent physicians searching for a disease that fitted the clues before them—routinely misdiagnosed the disease. Influenza did not fit the clues.

+

During the course of the epidemic, 47 percent of all deaths in the United States resulted from influenza and its complications. Nearly as many people died from influenza as from all other causes combined—including cancer, heart disease, stroke, tuberculosis, accidents, suicide, and murder. It killed enough to decrease the average life expectancy in the United States by more than ten years.

Some of those who died from influenza and pneumonia would have died even if no epidemic had occurred. Pneumonia was, after all, already a leading cause of death. So the key figure is actually the "excess death" toll. That means how many deaths *wouldn't* have happened had the epidemic not occurred. Investigators today believe that in the United States the 1918–19 epidemic caused an excess death toll of about 675,000 people. The nation then had a population between 105 and 110 million, while it was approximately 330 million in 2023. So a comparable figure today would be approximately 2 million deaths.

And there was something even beyond the numbers that gave the 1918 influenza pandemic terrifying immediacy and brought it into homes with the most life.

Influenza almost always selects the weakest in a society to kill, the very young and the very old. It almost always allows the most vigorous, the most healthy, to escape.

There was no such grace about influenza in 1918. It killed the young and strong. Studies worldwide all found the same thing. Unlike with COVID-19, well over 90 percent of the excess mortality occurred in people *younger* than sixty-five. Children under ten died in extraordinary numbers—at a rate roughly twenty times the deaths today from all causes combined for children in that age group. The second group most likely to die, again unlike COVID-19, was young adults, the healthiest and strongest part of the population. Those with the most to live for—the robust, the fit, the hearty, the ones raising young sons and daughters—those were the ones who died.

In the American military alone, influenza-related deaths totaled just over the number of Americans killed in combat in either World War I or the Vietnam War. But those most vulnerable of all to influenza, those most likely of the most likely to die, were pregnant women.

The 1918 influenza struck so suddenly that many victims could remember the precise instant they knew they were sick, so suddenly that throughout the world reports were common of people who toppled off horses, collapsed on the sidewalk. Death itself could come so fast.

✚

It was the lungs that had attracted attention from pathologists first. Physicians and pathologists had many times seen lungs of those dead of pneumonia. Many of the deaths, probably even most of them, occurred more than a week after the first symptoms from other, secondary bacterial infections appeared. The influenza virus destroyed the natural defenses in the nose, mouth, throat, and esophagus that are supposed to protect a body from infection. Without these defenses, bacteria marched unopposed into the lungs and grew. Even today, with antibiotics and modern intensive care units, bacterial pneumonia that's contracted after influenza kills between 6 and 8 percent of those infected.

The lungs of victims of these secondary bacterial infections looked at autopsy like those of victims of the normal pneumonias that pathologists had seen many times. But many of these victims died much more quickly, a few days and sometimes even the first day after symptoms appeared. They most likely died of an overwhelming and massive invasion of the virus itself in combination with the counterattack of the immune system. And the lungs of these victims who died quickly during the pandemic were different. They were filled with the debris of destroyed cells and with every element of the immune system, from enzymes to white blood cells. And they were filled with blood.

The immune system begins its defense far in advance of the lungs, with enzymes in saliva. Then it raises physical obstacles, such as nasal hairs that filter out large particles. If something does gain a foothold in the upper respiratory tract, the body first tries to flush it out with more fluid—hence the typical runny nose— and then expel it with coughs and sneezes. All these defenses work so well that the lungs themselves are normally sterile.

But when the lungs *do* become infected, other defenses, lethal and violent defenses, come into play. For the immune system is at its core a killing machine. It targets infecting organisms, attacking with a complex arsenal of weapons and neutralizing or killing the invaders.

In 1918 the virus was often so efficient at invading the lungs that the immune system had to mount a massive response to it. And so what was killing young adults a few days after the first symptom was *not* the virus. The killer was the massive immune response itself, which filled the lungs with fluid and debris, making it impossible for the exchange of oxygen to take place. The immune response killed. An army physician found that the only other causes that compared were those of a severe lung infection known as pneumonic plague or "those seen in acute death from poison gas."[2]

Seventy years after the pandemic, Edwin Kilbourne, a highly respected scientist who spent much of his life studying influenza, confirmed this observation, stating that the condition of the lungs was "unusual in other viral respiratory infections and is reminiscent of lesions seen following inhalation of poison gas."[3]

But the cause was not poison gas. It was only influenza.

Many who died in the 2009 swine flu pandemic died from the same cause. So did many who died from COVID-19, although in COVID-19 the process moved much more slowly.

But the 1918 virus didn't stop at destroying the lungs. Like COVID-19, it attacked and damaged virtually every organ. Upon autopsy, the brain showed "marked hyperemia"—blood flooding the brain, probably because of an out-of-control inflammatory response. Elsewhere "the brain tissues were noticeably dry."[4] The virus inflamed or affected the pericardium—the sac of tissue and fluid that protects the heart—and the heart muscle itself.

At least some damage to the kidneys "occurred in nearly every case."[5] The same was true for the liver. Muscles along the rib cage were torn apart both by the disease and by the stress of coughing, but many other muscles showed degeneration as well.

While the virus itself may well have caused some of this damage, the immune system definitely contributed—and probably caused most of it. In its attempt to kill the virus, the immune response was killing the host.

✚

As influenza spread from cantonments to cities, as it spread within cities, as it moved from city to town to village to farmhouse, medical science began moving as well. It began its own race against the pathogen, moving more rapidly and with more purpose than it ever had.

Scientists did not presume to think that they would or could control this rage of nature. But they did not abandon their search for ways to control the damage of this rage. They still tried to save lives. To save lives they needed the answer to at least one of three questions.

First, they needed to understand the *epidemiology* of influenza, meaning how it behaved and spread. Scientists had already learned to control cholera, typhoid, yellow fever, malaria, bubonic plague, and other diseases by understanding their epidemiology, even before developing either a vaccine or cure.

Second, they needed to learn its *pathology*, meaning what it did within the body, the precise course of the disease. That, too, might allow them to intervene in some way that saved lives.

Third, they needed to know what the pathogen was, what microorganism caused influenza. This could allow them to find a way to stimulate the immune system to prevent or cure the disease. It was also conceivable that even without knowing the precise cause, they could develop a serum or vaccine.

The easiest question to answer for influenza was its epidemiology. Most believed, correctly, that it was an airborne pathogen. Breathing it in could cause the disease. They did not know the details, like that, for example, when the virus floats in the air it can infect someone else for anywhere from an hour to a day after it is exhaled. Or that the lower the humidity, the longer the virus survives. But they did know that it was a disease spread most easily in crowds. They also had an accurate estimate that someone with influenza "sheds" the virus—can infect others—usually from the third to the sixth day after they are infected. (Although some victims, again as with COVID-19, shed virus even before they had symptoms.)

They also believed, correctly, that people could catch influenza not only by inhaling it but by hand-to-mouth or hand-to-nose contact. They rightly thought, for instance, that a sick person could cover their mouth with their hand when they coughed, then several hours later shake hands, and the second person could then rub their chin in thought or touch their nose or stick a piece of candy in their mouth and infect themselves. Similarly, someone sick could cough into a hand, touch a hard surface such as a doorknob, and spread it to someone else who turns the doorknob and later brings a hand to their face. In fact, the virus can remain infectious on a hard surface for days. They had this knowledge of influenza's epidemiology. But it wasn't enough to stop it.

Scientists were also learning too well about the pathology of the disease and its natural course. They were learning chiefly that they could do almost nothing to intervene in serious cases. They believed they could, however, possibly save lives if they could prevent or treat the slower moving pneumonias caused by what they were fairly quickly suspecting to be secondary bacterial infections.

They had tools, they could manipulate the immune system, they could prevent and cure some pneumonias . . . if they could find the pathogen.

✚

William Welch himself would not be the one to find the pathogen. Welch wasn't feeling very well. No doubt he tried to shrug off the discomfort. He had, after all, had an exceedingly difficult trip. From Camp Devens he took a train directly to Baltimore.

Just before going to Devens, he and others had concluded their latest round of camp inspections. They had taken a few days of relaxation in Asheville, North Carolina, and then been abruptly ordered to the surgeon general's office. They were sent straight on to Devens and there discovered this terrible disease.

So Welch had every reason to be tired and out of sorts. But as the train moved south he felt worse and worse. He likely looked at himself clinically, objectively, and made a correct diagnosis: he had influenza.

Welch did not go to the hospital. Almost seventy years old—forty years older than those who were dying in the greatest numbers—having just left the horror at Devens and knowing the enormous strain on and therefore the likely poor care he would receive even at the Hopkins facility, he later said, "I could not have dreamed of going to a hospital at that time."[6]

Instead, he went to bed immediately in his own rooms and stayed there. After ten days at home, when he felt well enough to travel, he moved to a favorite hotel in Atlantic City, New Jersey, where he stayed in bed for several more weeks recuperating. He had planned to attend a meeting on influenza at the Rockefeller Institute, but he canceled. He had not recovered enough to attend. He would play no further role in medical science for the course of the epidemic. He would not participate in the search for a solution. Welch's generation had transformed American medicine, but if further scientific breakthroughs were to be made, the next generation would be the one to do so.

✛

But other outstanding scientists were searching for a solution all across the United States. If the country was lucky, very lucky indeed, one of them might find something soon enough to help.

For all the urgency, investigators could not allow themselves to be panicked into a disorderly approach. Disorder would lead nowhere.

They began with what they knew and with what they could do.

They could kill pathogens outside the body. An assortment of chemicals could disinfect a room, or clothes, and they knew precisely the amount of chemicals needed. They knew how to disinfect instruments and materials. They knew how to grow bacteria and how to stain bacteria to make them visible under microscopes.

Yet in the midst of crisis, with death everywhere, none of that knowledge was useful. Medicine, at least, knew how to use one tool: the immune system itself.

Investigators understood the basic principles of the immune system. They knew how to manipulate those principles to prevent and cure some diseases. They knew how to grow and weaken or strengthen bacteria in the laboratory and how to stimulate an immune response in an animal. They knew how to make vaccines.

To have the best hope of protecting with a vaccine or curing with a serum, investigators needed to isolate the pathogen. They needed to answer a first question, the most important question—indeed, at this point the only question. What caused the disease?

CHAPTER ELEVEN

⌒⌇⌒

Bacillus influenzae

Certainty creates strength. Certainty gives one something upon which to lean. Uncertainty is scary. To be a scientist requires not only intelligence and curiosity but passion, patience, creativity, self-sufficiency, and courage. It is not just the courage to venture into the unknown. It is the courage to accept—indeed, embrace—uncertainty.

A scientist must accept the fact that all their work, even beliefs, may break apart upon a single laboratory finding. And just as Albert Einstein refused to accept his own theory until his predictions were tested, one must seek to test one's findings. Ultimately a scientist has nothing to believe in but the process of inquiry.

All real scientists exist on the frontier. The best among them move deep into areas where they know almost nothing, where the very tools and techniques needed do not exist, where the scientist must create . . . *everything*. It is tedious work that begins with figuring out what tools one needs and then making them. A shovel can dig up dirt but cannot penetrate rock. Would a pick then be best, or would dynamite be better? If the rock is impenetrable, if dynamite would destroy what one is looking for, is there another way of getting information about what the rock holds?

Ultimately, if the researcher succeeds, a flood of colleagues will pave roads over the path laid, and those roads will be orderly and straight, taking an investigator in minutes to a place the pioneer spent months or years looking for. And the perfect tool will be available for purchase.

One key to science is that work be *reproducible*. That is, some- one in another laboratory doing the same experiment will get the same result. The result then is reliable enough that someone else can build upon it. Because to be truly useful, a result must be able to be explored and expanded upon. One must be able to learn more from it and to use it as a foundation for future results.

✚

A German scientist named Richard Pfeiffer believed he had found the answer to the question of what caused influenza twenty-five years earlier. The scientific director of the Institute for Infectious Disease in Berlin and a general in the German army, Pfeiffer was sixty years old in 1918.

During and after the 1889–90 influenza pandemic, which had been the most severe influenza pandemic in three hundred years until the 1918 pandemic, Pfeiffer had searched for the cause. Carefully, painstakingly, he had isolated a type of bacteria from people suffering from influenza. He often found these bacteria the sole organism present, and he found them in "astonishing numbers."[1]

Pfeiffer was confident that what he had found was the cause of influenza. He even named the bacteria *Bacillus influenzae*. Among scientists, the bacteria quickly became known as "Pfeiffer's bacillus." His reputation gave his finding tremendous weight. Who would challenge him? Who would demand that his work be reproducible?

+

When the epidemic began, laboratories everywhere turned to investigating influenza. But by the fall of 1918 these laboratories could function only on a far-reduced scale. Research had been cut back and focused on war, on poison gas or defending against it, on preventing infection of wounds, on ways to prevent diseases that incapacitated troops.

As influenza stretched its fingers across the United States, virtually every serious medical scientist began looking for a cure. Most of them, simply, were not good enough to address the problem with any hope of success. They tried anyway. Their attempt was heroic. It required not just scientific ability but physical courage. They moved among the dead and dying, exposing themselves repeatedly to the pathogen that was killing more humans than any other in history.

Of all those working on it in the United States, perhaps the most important were Oswald Avery at the Rockefeller

Institute, William Park and Anna Williams at the New York City Department of Public Health, and Paul Lewis in Philadelphia.

On September 15, New York City's first influenza death occurred. In late August, William Park and Anna Williams had begun devoting all their energies to the disease. Park and Williams had collaborated for twenty-five years, and they complemented each other perfectly. He was a quiet, somewhat reserved man who involved himself directly with patients. What drove him was the desire to bring laboratory research to them.

Anna Williams, meanwhile, injected a certain wildness and creativity into the laboratory. She enjoyed going up in airplanes with stunt fliers—a reckless act in pre–World War I airplanes—and loved sudden fast turns and out-of-control drops. As a driver she was always speeding; when traffic was stalled, she often simply pulled into the opposite side of the road and proceeded, and she had a string of traffic tickets to prove it.

Despite—or more likely because of—her wildness, she had established herself as the premier woman medical scientist in America. Her achievement came at a price. She was unhappy. She was lonely. Still, in science, at least, she had thrills indeed.

Both Williams and Park were fifty-five years old in 1918. There were no thoughts of thrills on the long drive and rough roads from Manhattan to Camp Upton on Long Island, even though Williams was driving. At the camp the military doctors, knowing what was happening at Devens, begged for advice. But as yet Park and Williams had no advice to give; they could only swab the throats and nasal passages of the sick at Upton, return to their laboratory, and proceed.

There was nothing like Park's laboratory in the world. From the street outside, Park could look up with pride on the six-story building full of laboratories, knowing that his successes had built them. Streetcars, horse-drawn carriages, and automobiles clattered past, and the smell of manure mixed with that of gasoline and oil.

Inside the building, Park oversaw a virtual industry. More than two hundred workers reported to him, nearly half of them scientists or technicians. He loved the place; in fact, he loved it so much he donated his salary as professor of bacteriology at New York University to it.

His laboratory could function in extreme crisis. It had done so before: preventing outbreaks of cholera and typhoid, not only in New York City but all over the country; when requested, Park had sent teams to fight outbreaks of disease elsewhere.

And one other ability made the department unique. If a solution was found, Park's lab could produce serum and vaccines in industrial quantities as quickly as—and of better quality than—any drug manufacturer in the world. Park and Williams had done it once before. In 1894 they had discovered a way to make a diphtheria toxin five hundred times as powerful as that used by Europeans. This strength led to a far more efficient antitoxin and slashed the cost to one-tenth what it had been. The lab soon became the most reliable producer of the antitoxin in the world.

So it was not surprising that soon after Park returned from Camp Upton, he received a telegram from Richard Pearce, head of the National Research Council's section on medicine. Pearce wanted to know: "Will your lab undertake the necessary bacteriological studies and make reports as quickly as possible to the undersigned?"[2]

Park instantly wired back, "Will undertake work."[3] He was confident of victory. He intended to make the most thorough study of any disease outbreak ever. The workload would be enormous, but he believed that his department could handle it.

Within days, though, almost within hours, the disease began to overwhelm the department. As influenza struck first one janitor or technician or scientist at a time, then four at a time, then fifteen at a time, the laboratory reeled. Influenza humbled Park, and quickly.

Park was trying to get just one thing right, the important thing. If they found the pathogen, they could produce a vaccine against it. *What was the pathogen?*

✚

New York City was panicking.

Literally hundreds of thousands of people were sick simultaneously. It was impossible to get a doctor, and perhaps even more impossible to get a nurse. Reports came in that nurses were being held by force in the homes of patients too frightened and desperate to allow them to leave. Nurses were literally being kidnapped.

If Park was to have any impact on the course of the epidemic, he would have to guess—and guess right. His laboratory had only two constants. One was an endless supply of samples from live patients and organs from the dead. "We had plenty of material, I am sorry to say,"[4] Williams observed dryly. Their other constant was their routine. There was nothing even faintly exciting about this work; it was pure boredom. And yet every step involved contact with something that could kill. Each step took time, time while people died, but they had no choice.

The most tedious tasks mattered. Washing glassware mattered. Contaminated glassware could ruin an experiment, waste time, cost lives. In the course of this work, 220,488 test tubes, bottles, and flasks would be sterilized. Everything mattered, and yet no one knew who would report to work each day, who would not—and who would suddenly be carried across the street to the hospital.

Every step took time. Time that they did not have.

Four days after accepting the task from Pearce, Park wired, "The only results so far that are of real importance have been obtained in two fatal cases . . . There were absolutely no influenza bacilli in either of the lungs."[5]

The failure to find the influenza bacillus maddened Park. His best hope to produce a vaccine or serum would be to find a known pathogen, and the most likely suspect was the one Pfeiffer had named *Bacillus influenzae*. Pfeiffer had been and still was confident it caused the disease. Park had the utmost respect for Pfeiffer, but he would not hesitate to rule out *Bacillus influenzae* if he did not find good evidence for it. Working in these desperate circumstances, he wanted to confirm rather than reject Pfeiffer's work. He wanted the answer to be *Bacillus influenzae*.

While others in the lab searched for other organisms, Park asked Williams to concentrate on finding Pfeiffer's *Bacillus influenzae*. She did find it. She found it constantly.

Less than a week after first reporting his failure to find it, Park wired Pearce that *Bacillus influenzae* "would seem to be the starting point of the disease."[6] But Park felt that his methods had been less than thorough and added that there was still the possibility that some unknown virus "may be the starting point."

Still, the report had consequences, and Park's laboratory began the struggle to produce an antiserum and vaccine to it.

But the only way to know for certain that *Bacillus influenzae* caused the disease was to isolate the pathogen, use it to re-create the disease in an experimental animal, and then re-isolate the pathogen from the animal. The bacillus did kill laboratory rats. But their symptoms did not resemble influenza. Human experiments had begun. But none of the volunteer subjects had yet gotten sick. In a scientific sense, they still had very little to go on.

✛

While Park tried to produce an antiserum or vaccine against the disease in New York, Philadelphia was approaching collapse. Its experience would soon be echoed in many cities around the country.

There Paul Lewis was searching for the answer as well. Few, including Park, were more likely to find it. The son of a physician, Lewis grew up in Milwaukee, went to the University of Wisconsin, and finished his medical training at the University of Pennsylvania in 1904. Even before leaving medical school, he knew he intended to spend his life in the laboratory. He seemed born for it. It was the only place where he was happy; he loved not only the work itself but the environment, loved disappearing into the laboratory and into thought.

But now the city did not need laboratory breakthroughs that deepened understanding. It needed instant successes. He had only weeks, even days.

Most people who contracted the disease survived. Even most people who contracted pneumonia survived. It was quite possible that their blood and their serum—a liquid found within blood—held antibodies that would cure or prevent disease in others. Experiments began in Philadelphia using both the whole blood and serum of survivors of influenza. These were not scientific experiments, with a careful, meticulous design and controls; they were desperate attempts to save lives. If there was any sign this procedure worked, the science could follow later.

Lewis tried to develop an influenza vaccine using the same methods he had used once before. A decade earlier, working with his mentor Simon Flexner at the Rockefeller Institute, Lewis had proven that a virus caused polio. His discovery is still considered a landmark achievement in the history of virology—at the time, no one knew what a virus really was; they knew only that it was much smaller than the smallest bacteria. Lewis had then developed a vaccine that protected monkeys against polio with nearly 100 percent effectiveness.

Lewis stayed in his laboratory because research could find bacteria. He and everyone in his laboratories were working hours and days without relief, taking only a few hours off for sleep, running procedure after procedure, searching for bacteria. They worked twenty-four hours a day in shifts. And then they waited, frustrated by the time it took bacteria to grow. Frustrated by samples that became contaminated and unusable. Frustrated by everything that interfered with their progress.

In the first fifteen cases, Lewis found no *Bacillus influenzae*. Then, like Park and Williams, he adjusted his techniques and began to find it regularly. Lewis did not believe this meant he had solved the problem. True, he had isolated *Bacillus influenzae*. But he had also isolated pneumococcus. Some instinct pointed him in another direction. He shifted his experiments from trying to kill tuberculosis bacteria to trying to kill pneumococci.

But death surrounded him. Lewis turned his attention back to helping produce the only thing that might work *now*. So he chose as his targets the bacteria that he and others had found. In laboratories around the city, investigators no longer investigated. They leapfrogged steps and simply tried to produce one thing after another that logic suggested might work, which meant growing several different strains of bacteria and combining them into a vaccine. There was no certainty that anything they produced would work. There was only hope.

Lewis's laboratory had no ability to produce the immense quantities of vaccine needed. That required an industrial operation. He handed off this task to others in the city. It would take time to grow enough bacteria in cultures for tens of thousands of people.

The whole process, even in its most accelerated state, would take at least three weeks. And it would take time once they made the vaccine to administer it to thousands and thousands of people in a series of injections of increasingly strong doses spaced several days apart. In all that time, the disease would be killing. And while a vaccine could help prevent the disease, it would not be a cure.

Meanwhile, Lewis also began work on making a serum that could cure the disease. This work was trickier. A serum could aim at only one specific target; if it worked at all, it would work only against a single organism. Lewis chose as his single target *Bacillus influenzae.*

Lewis knew full well that little of what he was doing was good science. It was all, or nearly all, based on informed guesswork. He only worked harder.

✚

When Welch had first seen autopsies of victims at Camp Devens, he had called Oswald Avery at the Rockefeller Institute, asking him to get on the next train from New York. He hoped Avery could identify the pathogen killing the men at Devens.

Avery immediately left his own lab, walked the few blocks home for a change of clothes, then went to Grand Central Station. Late that afternoon he arrived at Devens and immediately began laboratory tests.

From the first, he encountered difficulties, getting puzzling results. He stayed at Devens long enough to grow cultures of bacteria. Like Park and Lewis, Avery had initial difficulty finding *Bacillus influenzae.* But then he began to find it.

Avery was not sure that *Bacillus influenzae* was the cause of the influenza at Devens, though. He based conclusions only upon his own findings. And his findings did not convince him yet. He'd found no sign of any bacterial invasion in seven cases. Also, in roughly half the cases he was finding both *Bacillus influenzae* and other organisms. He could interpret his findings in several ways, so he could not draw a single conclusion.

By early October, Avery was back at Rockefeller hearing reports from dozens of other investigators around the country and the world that they, too, were finding the influenza bacillus. But there were also reports of failures to find it. It would be easy to dismiss the failures to find it as failures of technique. Still, Avery's own findings left too many unanswered questions for him to reach a conclusion, crisis or not. Unlike Park, Williams, and Lewis, Avery was not ready to reach even a tentative conclusion. Yes, Pfeiffer's *Bacillus influenzae* might cause influenza. But he was not convinced.

Oswald Avery was an unusual individual. He dove deeply into a thing, to the deepest depths, following down the narrowest pathways and into the tiniest openings, leaving no loose ends. In every way his life was focused, narrow, controlled.

His personal office, adjacent to his laboratory, reflected focus as well. René Dubos, a prominent scientist, called it "small and bare, as empty as possible, without the photographs, mementos, pictures, unused books, and other friendly items that usually adorn and clutter a work place."[7]

For Avery did not wish to be disturbed. He was not rude or unkind or ungenerous. Far from it. But he burrowed in, deeper and deeper into the world of his own making, a world that he could define and over which he could exert some control.

But narrow did not mean small. There was nothing small about his thinking. When Avery experimented, a colleague said, "His attitude had many similarities with the hunter in search of his prey."[8] Avery had a hunter's patience. He could lie in wait for an hour, a day, a week, a month, a season. But he did not simply wait; he wasted not a single hour, he plotted, he observed, he learned.

At Rockefeller, Avery was hardly the only one devoting all his energies to influenza. Martha Wollstein, a respected bacteriologist who had studied influenza bacillus since 1905 and had years before collaborated on an unsuccessful effort to develop a serum for Pfeiffer's *Bacillus influenzae*, was searching for antibodies in the blood of recovered patients.

Everywhere the pressure was intense. Investigators struggled to find something—anything—that could help, that could contain the explosion. Though no one had found anything certain, laboratories were producing enough vaccines and serum for hundreds of thousands and perhaps millions of people.

Even in the midst of this death, this pressure, Avery would not be rushed. More and more reports came in that investigators around the world could not find the *Bacillus influenzae*. Perhaps technical errors prevented it being found. Or perhaps it was not present. In which case, what *was* causing the illness?

In his usual methodical way, Avery took the steps most likely to settle the question. He poured his energies into finding ways to make it easier to grow *Bacillus influenzae*. If he succeeded, then everyone could learn whether the inability to find the bacillus was because of incompetence or the absence of the bacteria.

Over a period of weeks, he made significant progress. Soon they would know that if *Bacillus influenzae* was not found it was because it was not there. But Avery would not discuss a conclusion he was not yet ready to support.

In the meantime, the killing continued.

PART IV

—— **+** ——

DEADLY DECISIONS

CHAPTER TWELVE

~ৡৣৎৣ৶

Confronting the Virus

The United States had entered the war with little preparation in April 1917, and mobilizing the country took time. By the summer of 1918, however, things looked very different. President Woodrow Wilson had created a Food Administration to control and distribute food, a Fuel Administration to ration coal and gasoline, and a War Industries Board to oversee the entire economy. He had taken greater control over the railroads and had created a federally sponsored river barge line that brought commerce back to life on the Mississippi River. He had built many dozens of military bases, each of which held at least tens of thousands of soldiers or sailors. He had created industries that made America's shipyards teem with hundreds of thousands of laborers launching hundreds of ships, and he had other workers dig new coal mines to produce coal.

Wilson had also created a vast propaganda machine, an internal spy network, and a war-bond-selling network that extended to the level of residential city blocks. He had even succeeded in stifling free speech, arresting and imprisoning powerful men, including radical labor leaders, editors of German-language newspapers, and even a congressman, some for prison terms longer than ten years.

He had injected the government into American life in ways unlike any other in the nation's history. And the final extension of federal power had come only in the spring of 1918, after the first wave of influenza had begun jumping from camp to camp. The government expanded the draft, requiring all eligible male citizens between the ages of eighteen and forty-five to enter into military service. On May 23, 1918, Provost Marshal Enoch Crowder, who oversaw the draft, had issued his "work or fight" order, stating that anyone not employed in an essential industry would be drafted—an order that caused major league baseball to shorten its season and sent many ballplayers scurrying for jobs that were "essential." Crowder promised that "all men within the enlarged age would be called within a year." *All* men, the government had said, with orders for an estimated thirteen million to register on September 12.

All this powerful and focused momentum of the war would not be turned or slowed easily. Not even by the prospect of peace. As the epidemic was gathering full steam in fall 1918, peace was only weeks away. At the end of September, a key German general urged his country's leader to end the war; the German army was close to collapsing. In the first week of October, both Austria and Germany separately sent inquiries about peace terms to the Allies. On October 7, Austria delivered a diplomatic note to

Wilson formally seeking peace on any terms Wilson chose. Ten days later—days filled with battle and deaths—the Austrian note remained unanswered. Instead Wilson pressed, pressed with all his might—and that meant all the nation's might.

He was now fighting to the death; he was fighting only to kill. *To fight you must be brutal and ruthless*, he had said. *Force!* he had demanded. *Force to the utmost!* There would be no letup in the powerful momentum he had created.

If Wilson and his government would not be turned by the prospect of peace, they would hardly be turned by a virus. Wilson took no public note of the disease, and the thrust of the government was not diverted. The relief effort for influenza victims would find no assistance in the Food Administration or the Fuel Administration or the Railroad Administration. From neither the White House nor any other senior administration post would there come any leadership, any attempt to set priorities, any attempt to coordinate activities, any attempt to deliver resources.

The military, especially the army, would confront the virus directly. But the military would give no help to civilians. Instead it would draw further upon civilian resources.

One person did take action, however. On September 26, although many training camps had not yet seen any influenza cases at all, Enoch Crowder canceled the next draft. And he would also cancel the draft after that one. It had been scheduled to send 142,000 men to the cantonments.

Canceling the draft was a bold move that likely saved thousands of lives, but Crowder did not do it to save lives. He did it because he recognized that the disease was utterly overwhelming and creating total chaos in the cantonments. There could be no training until the disease passed. Crowder's decision and the efforts of the Gorgas-led army medical corps would be the only bright spots in the response of the federal government.

If Wilson did nothing about influenza in the military, he did even less for civilians. He continued to say nothing publicly. There is no indication that he ever said anything privately, either. No hint that he so much as asked anyone in the government about efforts to fight the disease.

Wilson had appointed strong men to his administration, powerful men, and they took decisive actions. But none of those appointees had any real responsibility for health. Surgeon General Rupert Blue, head of the United States Public Health Service, did. And Blue was not a strong man.

Blue was physically strong, with a square face and a thick, athletic body. But he was not strong in ways that mattered, in leadership. After finishing his medical studies in 1892, Blue had immediately joined the Public Health Service and remained there his entire professional life.

When the war began, Wilson did not bother to choose a new surgeon general, but he did make the Public Health Service part of the military. Blue knew of the possibility of influenza in the United States, yet he made no preparations whatsoever to try to contain it. And he made no effort whatsoever to prepare the Public Health Service for a crisis.

It was not until September 13 that the Public Health Service made any public comment about the virus, when it stated, "Owing to disordered conditions in European countries, the bureau has no authoritative information as to the nature of the disease or its prevalence."[1] Later Blue defended himself for not taking more aggressive action. *This was influenza, only influenza*, he seemed to be saying.

On Saturday, September 21, the first influenza death occurred in Washington, DC. That same day, Camp Lee outside Petersburg, Virginia, had six deaths, while Camp Dix in New Jersey saw thirteen soldiers and one nurse die. Still Blue did little. On Sunday, September 22, the Washington, DC, newspapers reported that Camp Humphreys (now Fort Belvoir), just outside the city, had sixty-five cases.

Now, finally, in a box next to those reports, the local papers published the government's first warning of the disease:

Surgeon General's Advice to Avoid Influenza

Avoid needless crowding . . .

Smother your coughs and sneezes . . .

Your nose not your mouth was made to breathe thru . . .

Remember the 3 Cs, clean mouth, clean skin, and clean clothes . . .

Food will win the war . . . help by choosing and chewing your food well . . .

Wash your hands before eating . . .

Don't let the waste products of digestion accumulate . . .

Avoid tight clothes, tight shoes, tight gloves—seek to make nature your ally not your prisoner . . .

When the air is pure breathe all of it you can—breathe deeply.[2]

Such generalizations hardly reassured a public that knew that the disease was marching from army camp to army camp, killing soldiers in large numbers. Three days later, a second influenza death occurred in Washington, DC; also that day, senior medical personnel of the army, navy, and Red Cross met in Washington to try to figure out how they could aid individual states. Neither Blue nor a representative of the Public Health Service attended the meeting. Twenty-six states were by then reporting influenza cases.

Blue had still not laid plans for an organization to fight the disease. Perhaps he considered any further action outside the authority of the Public Health Service. But governors and mayors were demanding help, begging everyone in Washington for help.

Doctors and nurses were needed. As the disease spread, as warnings poured in, Congress acted. Without the delay of hearings or debate, it gave one million dollars to the Public Health Service. The money was enough for Blue to hire five thousand doctors for emergency duty for a month—if he could somehow find five thousand doctors worth hiring.

The Red Cross did not get government funds or direction, yet it had already allocated money to fight the epidemic and had begun organizing its own effort to do so—and do so on a massive scale. Its nursing department had already started mobilizing "home defense nurses": fully professional nurses, all of them women, who could not serve in the military because of age, disability, or marriage.

The Red Cross had separated the country into thirteen divisions, and the nursing committee chief of each one had already been told to find all people with any nursing training, not only professionals or those who had dropped out of nursing schools—for the Red Cross checked with all nursing schools—but down to and including anyone who had ever taken a Red Cross course in caring for the sick at home.

Finally, Blue began to organize the Public Health Service as well. But by then the virus had spanned the country. It was penetrating Alaska. It had crossed the Pacific to Hawaii. It had surfaced in Puerto Rico. It was about to explode across western Europe, across India, across China, across Africa as well.

✚

Nothing could have stopped the sweep of influenza through either the United States or the rest of the world—but ruthless intervention and quarantines might have interrupted its progress and created some relief in the spread. Action as strict as that taken in 2003 to contain the outbreak of a new disease called severe acute respiratory syndrome (the first SARS virus) could well have had an effect. Influenza, like COVID-19, could not have been contained as the first SARS was. Influenza is far more contagious. But any interruption in influenza's spread could have had significant impact, for the virus was growing weaker over time; somewhat less lethal variants seemed to be emerging. Simply delaying its arrival in a community or slowing its spread once there—just such minor successes—would have saved many, many thousands of lives.

There was precedent for ruthless action. Only two years earlier in 1916, several East Coast cities had fought a polio outbreak with the strictest measures. Public health authorities wherever polio threatened had been relentless. But that was before the United States entered the war. For influenza now, nearly all cities closed schools, theaters, saloons, and churches and banned public gatherings, but with the need to produce material for war, few cities took any actions against businesses.

The Public Health Service and the Red Cross still had a single chance to accomplish something of consequence. By early October, the first fall outbreaks, along with those that had happened in the spring, already suggested that the virus attacked in a cycle: it took roughly six weeks from the appearance of the first cases for the epidemic to peak and then decline in civilian areas. So Red Cross and Public Health Service planners expected that the virus would peak in different parts of the country at different times. During the height of the epidemic, individual communities would be utterly overwhelmed. But if the Red Cross and Public Health Service could concentrate doctors, nurses, and supplies in one community when most needed, they might be able to withdraw that aid as the disease ebbed and shift it to the next area in need, and the next.

The Public Health Service would find, pay, and assign all physicians. It would decide when and where to send nurses and supplies and to whom nurses would report, and it would deal with state and local public health authorities. The Red Cross would find and pay nurses, furnish emergency hospitals with medical supplies wherever local authorities could not, and take responsibility for virtually everything else that came up, including distributing information. The Red Cross did stipulate one limit on its responsibility: it would not meet requests from military camps. This stipulation was immediately forgotten; even the Red Cross soon gave the military precedence over civilians.

✚

Investigators around the country had developed various vaccines and sera by October of 1918. Doctors now had drugs that allevi-ated some symptoms or stimulated the heart, major hospitals had X-rays that could aid in diagnosis, and some hospitals had begun administering oxygen to help victims breathe.

Yet for a doctor to use these resources, any of them, that doctor had to have them—and also had to have time. The physical resources were hard to come by, but time was harder. A serum that might have helped against a secondary bacterial infection needed to be administered with precision and in numerous doses. There was no time. Not with patients overflowing wards, filling cots in hallways and on porches, not with doctors themselves fall-ing ill and filling those cots. Even if they had resources, they had no time.

Finding the doctors themselves was not easy. The military had already taken at least one-fourth—in some areas it was as much as one-third—of all the physicians and nurses. And the army, itself under violent attack from the virus, would lend none of its doctors to civilian communities no matter how desperate the circumstances.

That left approximately one hundred thousand doctors in a labor pool to draw from—but it was a pool limited in quality.

The virus was penetrating everywhere, doctors were needed everywhere, and no responsible doctor would abandon his (or, in a few instances, her) own patients in desperate need. In addition, the federal government was paying only fifty dollars a week—not a great salary even in 1918.

What could help, more than doctors, was nurses. Nursing could ease the strains on a patient; keep a patient hydrated, resting, calm; provide the best nutrition; cool the intense fevers. Nursing could give a victim of the disease the best possible chance to survive. Nursing could save lives.

But nurses were harder to find than doctors. There were one-quarter fewer, to begin with. Jane Delano's rejection of the 1912 attempt to create "practical nurses" for the military had meant that no reserve force of nursing aides existed. Gorgas's plan had been to produce thousands of such aides; instead, the Army School of Nursing had been established. So far it had produced only 221 student nurses and not a single graduate nurse.

Then, just before the epidemic struck, combat had intensified in France, and with it, so had the army's need for nurses. The Red Cross had already been recruiting nurses for the military with vigor. Each division, each chapter within a division, was given a quota. Red Cross professionals knew that their careers were at risk if they did not meet it. Recruiters had a list of all nurses in the country and their jobs and locations.

The drive was succeeding; it was removing from civilian life a huge proportion of nurses. The drive was succeeding so well that it all but stripped hospitals of their workforce.

One Red Cross recruiter wrote, "The work at National Headquarters has never been so difficult and is now overwhelming us . . . [We are searching] from one end of the United States to the other to rout out every possible nurse from her hiding place . . . There will be no nurses left in civil life if we keep on at this rate."[3]

The recruiter wrote that on September 5 and so couldn't know that in just three more days the virus would explode at Camp Devens, taking even more medical professionals away from the ordinary people who needed them.

CHAPTER THIRTEEN

ᖇᕼᕐ

Desperation

No doctors recruited by the Public Health Service were sent to Philadelphia. No nurses recruited by the Red Cross were sent there, either. Those institutions gave no help.

Each day, people discovered that friends and neighbors who had been perfectly healthy a week—or a day—earlier were dead. *What should I do?* People were panicked, desperate. *How long will it go on?*

At the time, Philadelphia was one of the most corrupt cities in the country; its mayor was indicted on three unrelated charges, including conspiracy to murder. He had done absolutely nothing to help in the pandemic. The entire city government had done nothing. Wilmer Krusen, head of the city health department, no longer had the confidence of anyone. Someone had to do *something*.

Paul Lewis felt the pressures. Finding *Bacillus influenzae* had begun his real work, not concluded it. Never had he been so consumed with the laboratory. He had started his experiments with the pneumococcus. He had continued to look at the influenza bacillus. He and others had developed a vaccine. He was trying to make a serum. All of these he did simultaneously, for the one thing he did not have was time. No one had time.

Of all the major cities in the United States, Philadelphia had the largest percentage of native-born citizens and, compared to New York, Chicago, Boston, Detroit, Buffalo, and other similar cities, the lowest percentage of immigrants. Philadelphia was not unusual in that its oldest and wealthiest families controlled the charities, the social service organizations—including the local Red Cross—and the state chapter of the Council of National Defense, a national entity created in 1916 to coordinate industries in case of war. But now, with the local government all but nonexistent, the city was unusual in that these families considered it their duty to use the Council of National Defense to take charge.

The Pennsylvania council retained extraordinary, although almost entirely unofficial, influence over everything from railroad schedules to profits and wages at every large company in the state. It held this power chiefly because it was headed by George Wharton Pepper.

An attorney who sat on the boards of half a dozen of the country's largest companies, Pepper had many abilities, and he knew how to command. He was the bluest of blue bloods; his great-great-grandfather had led the state militia in the Revolutionary War. Pepper's wife was a descendant of Benjamin Franklin.

Elizabeth Martin, the wife of a prominent judge, headed the council's Women's Division as well as Emergency Aid, the most important private social agency in the city. Nearly all the social agencies were run by women, strong women of intelligence and energy who were born to a certain rank but excluded from all pursuits beside charity. The mayor had created a committee of society women to respond to emergencies; it included Pepper's wife. But with city officials doing nothing whatsoever about the epidemic, the women resigned, effectively dissolving the committee. As Elizabeth Martin wrote the mayor, "Your committee has no real purpose . . . I therefore hereby sever my connection with it."[1]

Now, in place of the city government, Pepper, the Martins, and their colleagues summoned the heads of a dozen private organizations on October 7. And the women took charge, with Pepper adding his weight to theirs. They had already organized nearly the entire city to sell war bonds, all the way down to the level of each block, making each residential block the responsibility of "a logical leader no matter what her nationality"—i.e., an Irishwoman in an Irish neighborhood, an African American woman in an African American neighborhood, and so on.

They intended to use that same organization now to distribute everything from medical care to food. They intended to inject organization and leadership into chaos and panic. In conjunction with the Red Cross—which here, unlike nearly everywhere else in the country, allowed its own efforts to be incorporated into this larger effort—they also appealed for nurses, declaring, "The death toll for one day in Philadelphia alone was greater than the death toll from France for the whole American army for one day."[2]

The state Council of National Defense had already compiled a list of every physician in Pennsylvania, including those not practicing. Martin's unofficial committee begged each one on the list for help. The committee had money, and access to more money, to pay for the help. It set up a twenty-four-hour telephone bank for information and referrals. It transformed kitchens in public schools—which were closed—into soup kitchens that prepared meals for tens of thousands of people too ill to prepare their own. It divided the city into seven districts and, to conserve physicians' time, dispatched them according to geography, meaning that doctors did not see their own patients.

And it became a place that volunteers could come to. Nearly five hundred people offered to use their own cars either as ambulances or to chauffeur doctors—they were supplied with green flags that gave them right-of-way over all other vehicles. The organizers of the Liberty Loan drive diverted another four hundred cars to help. Thousands of individuals called the headquarters and offered to do what was needed.

Wilmer Krusen had not attended the October 7 meeting of the private groups and had been slow to act before. Now he changed. Perhaps the deaths finally changed him. Perhaps the fact that someone else was taking charge forced him to move. Whatever it was, he seemed suddenly not to care about bureaucracy or his own power. He just wanted to stop the disease.

He gave the group control over all nurses, hundreds of them, who worked for the city. He seized—in violation of the city charter—the city's $100,000 emergency fund and another $25,000 from a war emergency fund and used the money to supply emergency hospitals and hire physicians, paying them double what the Public Health Service was offering. He sent those physicians to every police station in South Philadelphia, the hardest-hit section. He wired the army and navy asking that no Philadelphia physicians be drafted until the epidemic slowed and that those who had already been drafted but had not yet reported to duty be allowed to remain in Philadelphia, because "the death rate for the past week [was] the largest in records of city."[3]

Under the initial burst of energy the city seemed to rally, to respond with vigor and courage now that leadership and organization seemed in place. But the epidemic did not slow. In virtually every home, someone was ill. People were already avoiding each other, turning their heads away if they had to talk, isolating themselves. The telephone company increased the isolation: with eighteen hundred telephone company employees out, the phone company allowed only emergency calls; operators listened to calls randomly and cut off phone service of those who made routine calls. And the isolation increased the fear. One survivor of the pandemic recalled, "They stopped people from communicating, from going to churches, closed the schools . . . closed all the saloons . . . Everything was quiet."[4]

Very likely half a million—possibly more—Philadelphians fell sick. It is impossible to be more precise: despite the new legal requirement to report cases, physicians were far too busy to do so, and by no means did physicians see all victims. Nor did nurses.

People needed help, and, despite the efforts of the committees, the Council of National Defense, and the Red Cross, help was impossible to get.

It seemed as if there had never been life before the epidemic. The disease informed every action of every person in the city. The archbishop released nuns for service in hospitals, including Jewish hospitals, and allowed them to violate rules of their orders, to spend overnights away from the convent, to break vows of silence. They did not make a dent in the need.

By then many of those who had earlier rushed forward to volunteer had withdrawn. The work was too gruesome or too difficult, or they themselves fell ill. Or they, too, were frightened. Every day, newspapers carried new and increasingly desperate pleas for volunteers. Krusen declared, "It is the duty of every well woman in the city who can possibly get away from her duties to volunteer for this emergency."

But who listened to him anymore?

Elizabeth Martin called for help from "all persons with two hands and a willingness to work."[5]

Few came.

On October 13, the Bureau of Child Hygiene publicly begged for neighbors to take in, at least temporarily, children whose parents were dying or dead. The response was almost nonexistent. The need was not only for medical care but for care itself. Entire families were ill and had no one to feed them.

The professionals had continued to do their duty. Doctors died, and others kept working. Nurses died, and others kept working. Others did their jobs as well. The police performed with heroism.

But citizens in general had largely stopped responding to pleas.

Fear began to break down the community of the city. Trust broke down, too. How could trust survive when people were lied to, when—even while publishing pleas for volunteers—newspapers constantly tried to reassure that all was well? One of the newspapers said this "is not a public health order . . . You have no cause for panic or alarm." People knew they were being lied to. Trust in authority disintegrated. The lies reassured no one, only increased the fear.

Susanna Turner, who did volunteer at an emergency hospital and stayed, who went there day after day, remembered,

> *The fear in the hearts of the people just withered them . . . They were afraid to go out, afraid to do anything . . . You just lived from day to day, did what you had to do and not think about the future . . . If you asked a neighbor for help, they wouldn't do so because they weren't taking any chances. If they didn't have it in their house, they weren't going to bring it in there . . . You didn't have the same spirit of charity that you do with a regular time, when someone was sick you'd go and help them, but at that time they helped themselves. It was a horror-stricken time.*[6]

In a normal week in Philadelphia, deaths from all causes combined—cancer, heart disease, accidents, murders and suicides, tuberculosis, *everything*—averaged 485. During the week of October 16 alone, 4,597 Philadelphians died from influenza or pneumonia, and influenza killed still more indirectly. That would be the worst week of the epidemic. But no one knew that at the time. Krusen had too often said the peak had passed. The press had too often spoken of triumph over disease.

+

What was happening in Philadelphia was happening everywhere. The US government was giving no guidance that the average person would find useful. Few local governments did better. They left a vacuum. Fear filled it.

The government's very efforts to preserve morale fostered the fear. Since the war began, morale—defined in the narrowest, most shortsighted fashion—had taken precedence in every public statement. As California senator Hiram Johnson said in 1917, "The first casualty when war comes is truth."[7]

It was a time when the phrase "brisk fighting" actually meant that more than 50 percent of a unit was killed or wounded, a time when the memoir of a nurse at the front, published in 1916, was pulled from shelves by her publisher after America entered the war because she told the truth about gruesome conditions.

Newspapers reported on the disease with the same mixture of truth and half truth, truth and distortion, truth and lies with which they reported everything else. And no national official ever publicly acknowledged the danger of influenza.

As terrifying as the disease was, the press made it more so. For what officials and the press said bore no relationship to what people saw and touched and smelled and endured. People could not trust what they read. Uncertainty follows distrust, fear follows uncertainty, and, under conditions such as these, terror follows fear.

Over and over in hundreds of newspapers, day after day, repeated in one form or another was Surgeon General Rupert Blue's reassurance: "There is no cause for alarm if precautions are observed."[8] Fear, that was the enemy. Yes, fear. And the more officials tried to control it with half truths and outright lies, the more the terror spread.

How could one not get panicky? Even before people's neighbors began to die, before bodies began to pile up in each new community, the information people saw all around them did not match the newspaper accounts they read.

In 1918 fear drove the people, and the government and the press could not control it. They could not control it because every true report had been diluted with lies. And the more the officials and newspapers reassured, the more they said *There is no cause for alarm if proper precautions are taken* or *Influenza is nothing more or less than old-fashioned grippe*, the more people believed themselves cast adrift on an ocean of death with no one to trust.

So people watched the virus approach, and feared. It was a thousand miles away, five hundred miles away, fifty miles away, twenty miles away. The virus had moved west and south from the East Coast by water and rail. It attacked cities and towns, reached into villages and small settlements, found its way even to isolated homes. It spread everywhere, varying in depth but covering everything, settling over the land in a great leveling. The war was something *over there*. The epidemic was *here*.

"Even if there was war," recalled Susanna Turner of Philadelphia, "the war was removed from us, you know . . . on the other side . . . This malignancy, it was right at our very doors."[9]

Washington, DC, resident William Sardo said, "It kept people apart . . . It took away all your community life; you had no community life, you had no school life, you had no church life, you had nothing . . . It completely destroyed all family and community life. People were afraid to kiss one another, people were afraid to eat with one another, they were afraid to have anything that made contact because that's how you got the flu . . . It destroyed those contacts and destroyed the intimacy that existed amongst people . . . You were constantly afraid."[10]

In Norwood, Massachusetts, a historian years later interviewed survivors. One man, a newsboy in 1918, remembered that his manager would "tell me to put the money on the table and he'd spray the money before he'd pick it up." Said another survivor, "There wasn't much visiting . . . We stayed by ourselves."[11]

The Red Cross reported incidents of the sick starving to death because no one had the courage to bring them food. People stayed by themselves indeed.

CHAPTER FOURTEEN

❧

Failed Efforts

The *Journal of the American Medical Association* repeatedly—sometimes twice in the same issue—published an "urgent call on physicians for help in localities where the epidemic is unusually severe . . . This service is just as definite a patriotic privilege as is that of serving in the medical corps of the army or navy . . . As the call is immediate and urgent it is suggested that any physician who feels that he can do some of this work telegraph to the Surgeon General, USPHS, Washington, DC."[1]

There were never enough.

Meanwhile, physicians attempted everything—*everything*—to save lives. They could relieve some symptoms. Doctors could address pain with everything from aspirin to morphine. They could control coughing at least somewhat with codeine and, said some, heroin. They gave oxygen.

Some treatment attempts that went beyond symptomatic relief had solid science behind them, even if no one had ever applied that science to influenza.

And there were treatments less grounded in science. They sounded logical. They *were* logical. But the reasoning was also desperate, the reasoning of a doctor ready to try anything, the reasoning that mixed wild ideas or thousands of years of practice with a few decades of scientific method. First-rate medical journals rejected articles about the most outlandish and ridiculous so-called therapies, but they published anything that at least seemed to make sense. There was no time for peer review, the standard evaluation process of scientific work by others in the field, no time for careful analysis.

Physicians injected people with typhoid vaccine, thinking—or simply hoping—it might somehow boost the immune system in general even though the specificity of the immune response was well understood. Some claimed the treatment worked. Others poured every known vaccine into patients on the same theory. Quinine was a medication that worked on one disease: malaria. Many physicians gave it for influenza with no better reasoning than desperation.

Others convinced themselves a treatment cured regardless of results. A Montana physician reported to *The New York Medical Journal* of his experimental treatment, "The results have been favorable." He had tried the treatment on six people; two died. Still he insisted, "In the four cases that recovered the results were immediate and certain."[2]

It was no different elsewhere in the world. Hundreds of millions—very likely tens of millions in the United States alone—saw no doctor, saw no nurse, but tried every kind of folk medicine or fraudulent remedy available or imaginable. Mothballs and garlic hung around people's necks. Others gargled with disinfectants, let frigid air sweep through their homes, or sealed windows shut and overheated rooms.

Advertisements filled the newspapers, sometimes set in the same small type as—and difficult to distinguish from—news articles, and sometimes set in large fonts blaring across a page. The one thing they shared was this: they all declared with confidence there *was* a way to stop influenza, there *was* a way to survive. Some claims were as simple as a shoe store's advertising, ONE WAY TO KEEP THE FLU AWAY IS TO KEEP YOUR FEET DRY. Some were as complex as MAKING A KOLYNOS GAS MASK TO FIGHT SPANISH INFLU-ENZA WHEN EXPOSED TO INFECTION.[3]

They all played to fear.

✚

By the middle of October, vaccines prepared by the best scientists were appearing everywhere. On October 17, Royal Copeland, head of the New York City Health Department, announced that Park's vaccine "had been tested sufficiently to warrant its recommendation as a preventive agency."[4] Copeland assured the public that "virtually all persons vaccinated with it [were] immune to the disease."

In Philadelphia on October 19, C. Y. White, a bacteriologist with the municipal laboratory, delivered ten thousand doses of a vaccine based on Paul Lewis's work, with tens of thousands of doses more soon to come. That same day, a new issue of *JAMA* appeared, thick with information about influenza. It included a preliminary evaluation of the experience of the vaccines in Boston. While it was found that the vaccines could not cure, "the statistical evidence, so far as it goes, indicates that the use of the vaccine"[5] had "some" value when it came to preventing disease. It was not a ringing endorsement, but at least it provided a little hope.

The Public Health Service made no effort to produce or distribute any vaccine or treatment for civilians. It received requests enough. It had nothing to offer.

The Army Medical School in Washington, DC, did mount a massive effort to make a vaccine. They needed one. At the army's own Walter Reed Hospital, the death rate for those with complicating pneumonia had reached 52 percent. On October 25, the vaccine was ready. The surgeon general's office informed all camp physicians, "The value of vaccination against certain of the more important organisms giving rise to pneumonia may be considered to be established . . . The army now has available for all officers, enlisted men, and civilian employees of the army a lipo vaccine containing pneumococcus Types I, II, and III."[6]

The army distributed two million doses of this vaccine in the next weeks. This marked an enormous production triumph. Earlier a prominent British scientist had pronounced it impossible for the British government to produce even forty thousand doses on short notice. But the vaccine still protected only against pneumonias caused by Type I and II pneumococci, and it came too late; by then the disease had already passed through nearly all cantonments. When civilian physicians from New York to California begged for the vaccine from the army, the reply came back that the army had in fact produced "a vaccine for the prevention of pneumonia, but none is available for distribution."

A cautionary *JAMA* editorial stated, "Unfortunately we as yet have no specific serum or other specific means for the cure of influenza, and no specific vaccine for its prevention."[7] Nearly every issue contained a similar warning: "Nothing should be done by the medical profession that may arouse unwarranted hope among the public and be followed by disappointment and distrust of medical science and the medical profession."[8]

JAMA represented the American Medical Association. AMA leaders had worked for decades to bring scientific standards and professionalism to medicine. They had only recently succeeded. They did not want to destroy the trust only recently established. They did not want medicine to become the mockery it had been not so long before.

In the meantime, physicians continued to try the most desperate measures. Vaccines were produced in great numbers—eighteen different kinds in Illinois alone. No one had any real idea whether any would work. They had only hope.

No medicine and none of the vaccines developed then could prevent influenza. The masks worn by millions were almost useless as designed—made of thin gauze and usually not secured tightly around the mouth and nose—and could not prevent a wearer from getting influenza. Only avoiding exposure to the virus could prevent it.

To this day, nothing can cure influenza, although vaccines can provide significant—but nowhere near complete—protection, and several antiviral drugs can reduce its severity.

Places that isolated themselves—such as a few military installations on islands—escaped. But the closing orders that most cities issued could not prevent exposure; they were not extreme enough. Shuttering saloons and theaters and churches meant nothing if significant numbers of people continued to climb onto streetcars, continued to go to work, continued to go to the grocer. Even where fear closed down businesses, where both store owners and customers refused to stand face-to-face and left orders on sidewalks, there was still too much interaction to break the chain of infection. The virus was too efficient, too explosive, too good at what it did. In the end, the virus did its will around the world.

✚

The virus pierced the ice of the Arctic and climbed the roadless mountains of Kentucky. It also penetrated the jungle. Among Americans and Europeans, the heaviest blows fell upon young adults densely packed together, civilian or military.

In Frankfurt, Germany, the mortality rate of all those hospitalized with influenza was 27.3 percent. In Paris, the government closed only schools, fearing that anything else would hurt morale. The death rate there was 10 percent of influenza victims and 50 percent of those who developed any complications.

And populations whose immune systems had seen few if any

influenza viruses of any kind were not just decimated but sometimes annihilated. This was true of Native Americans, of Pacific Islanders, of Africans.

In Cape Town and several other cities in South Africa, influenza would kill 4 percent of the entire population within four weeks of the first reported cases. 32 percent of white South Africans and 46 percent of black South Africans would be attacked. 0.82 percent of white Europeans in Cape Town would die, along with at least 2.72 percent—but likely a far, far higher percentage—of black Africans.

In Mexico, the virus swarmed through the dense population centers and through the jungles, overwhelming occupants of mining camps.

The virus ripped through Senegal, Sierra Leone, Spain, and Switzerland.

In Brazil, Rio de Janeiro suffered an attack rate of 33 percent.

In Buenos Aires, Argentina, the virus attacked nearly 55 percent of the population.

In Japan, it attacked more than one-third of the population.

The virus would kill 7 percent of the entire population in much of Russia and Iran.

In Guam, 10 percent of the population would die.

A few—*very* few—isolated locations around the world, where it was possible to impose a rigid quarantine and where authorities did so ruthlessly, escaped the disease entirely. American Samoa was one such place. There not a single person died of influenza.

Huge but unknown numbers died in China. In Chongqing, a

city in southwestern China, half the population was ill.

And yet the most terrifying numbers would come from India. As elsewhere in the world, India had suffered a spring wave. As elsewhere, this spring wave was relatively mild. In September influenza returned to Bombay (now Mumbai). As elsewhere, it was no longer mild.

Yet India was not like elsewhere. There influenza would take on truly killing dimensions. The case mortality rate for influenza reached 10.3 percent. In the Indian subcontinent alone, it is likely that close to twenty million died, and quite possibly the death toll exceeded that number.

Victor Vaughan, an influential colleague of William Welch, sitting in the office of the surgeon general of the army and head of the army's Division of Communicable Diseases, watched the virus move across the earth. A sober, serious scientist not given to overstatement, he wrote, "If the epidemic continues its mathematical rate of acceleration, civilization could easily disappear . . . from the face of the earth within a matter of a few more weeks."[9]

✚

Some diseases depend upon human civilization for their own existence. Measles is one example. Since a single exposure to measles usually gives lifetime immunity, the measles virus cannot find enough susceptible individuals in small towns to survive; without a new human generation to infect, the virus dies out. Epidemiologists have computed that measles requires an unvaccinated population of at least half a million people living in fairly close contact to continue to exist.

The influenza virus is different. Since birds provide a natural home for it, influenza does not depend upon civilization. In terms of its own survival, it would not matter if humans existed or not.

After it first jumped from an animal host to humans, as it passed from person to person it adapted to its new host species. It became increasingly efficient in its ability to infect and changed from the virus that caused a generally mild first wave of disease in the spring of 1918 to the lethal and explosive killer of the second wave in the fall. Once this happened, once it achieved near-maximum efficiency, two other natural processes came into play.

One process involved immunity. Once the virus passed through a population, that population developed at least some immunity to it. In a city or town, the cycle from the first case to the end of a local epidemic in 1918 generally ran six to eight weeks. In the army camps, with the men packed so densely, the cycle took usually three to four weeks.

Individual cases continued to occur after that, but the explosion of disease ended, and it ended abruptly. A graph of cases would look like the shape of a bell chopped off almost like a cliff just after the peak, with new cases suddenly dropping to next to nothing. After Philadelphia experienced its worst week of the pandemic on October 16, when the disease killed 4,597 people, new cases dropped sharply only ten days later. The city went from being ripped apart by the virus, emptying the streets and sparking rumors of the plague, to, on October 26, lifting the order closing public places. This all happened in the span of just ten days. By November 11, influenza had almost entirely disappeared from Philadelphia. The virus burned through available fuel. Then it quickly faded away.

The second process occurred within the virus. By nature, the influenza virus is dangerous, considerably more dangerous than the common aches and fever lead people to believe, but it does not kill routinely as it did in 1918. The 1918 pandemic reached an extreme unknown in any other widespread influenza outbreak in history.

The 1918 virus, like all influenza viruses, like all viruses that form mutant swarms, mutated rapidly. In mathematics, there is a rule of probability that states that an extreme event is likely to be followed by a less extreme event. The 1918 virus stood at an extreme. Any mutations were likely to make it less lethal rather than more lethal. In general, that is what happened. So just as it seemed that the virus would bring civilization to its knees, would do what the plagues of the Middle Ages had done, the virus instead mutated toward the behavior of most influenza viruses. As time went on, it became less lethal.

This first became apparent in army cantonments in the United States. Of the twenty largest cantonments, the first five attacked saw roughly 20 percent of all soldiers who caught influenza develop pneumonia. And 37.3 percent of the soldiers who developed pneumonia died. The worst numbers came from Camp Sherman in Ohio, which suffered the highest percentage of soldiers killed and was one of the first camps hit.

In the last five camps attacked, on average three weeks later, only 7.1 percent of influenza victims developed pneumonia. And only 17.8 percent of the soldiers who developed pneumonia died.

One alternative explanation to this improvement is that army doctors simply got better at preventing and treating pneumonia. But scientists and epidemiologists looked hard for any evidence of that. They found none. Nothing affected the course of the disease or changed it except the virus itself. The later the disease attacked, the less vicious the blow.

Inside each camp the same pattern held true. Soldiers struck down in the first ten days or two weeks died at much higher rates than soldiers in the same camp struck down late in the epidemic or after the epidemic actually ended.

Similarly, the first cities invaded by the virus—Boston, Baltimore, Pittsburgh, Philadelphia, Louisville, New York, New Orleans, and smaller cities hit at the same time—all suffered grievously. In those same places, the people infected later in the epidemic were not becoming as ill, and were not dying at the same rate as those infected in the first two to three weeks. Cities struck later in the epidemic also usually had lower mortality rates. As a comprehensive 1927 study of the pandemic observed, "In the later stages of the epidemic" some supposedly typical symptoms "were less frequently found," secondary bacterial infections were "more plainly recognizable, and the differences of locality were sharply marked . . . in 1919 the 'water-logged' lungs were relatively rarely encountered."[10]

The virus was never completely consistent. But, in general,

places hit later tended to be hit more mildly. San Antonio suffered one of the highest attack rates but lowest death rates in the country; the virus there infected 53.5 percent of the population, and 98 percent of all homes in the city had at least one person sick with influenza. But there the virus had mutated toward mildness; only 0.8 percent of those who got influenza died. (This death rate was still double that of normal influenza.)

The virus itself, more than any treatment provided, determined who lived and who died. The East Coast and the South, hit earliest, were hit the hardest. The West Coast was hit less hard. And the middle of the country suffered the least.

By late November 1918, with few exceptions, the virus had made its way around the world. The second wave was over, and the world was exhausted. But the virus, even as it lost some of its strength, was not yet finished.

✦

Only weeks after the disease seemed to have dissipated, when town after town had congratulated itself on surviving it—and in some places where people had had the arrogance to believe they had defeated it—after health boards and emergency councils had canceled orders to close theaters, schools, and churches and to wear masks, a third wave broke over the earth.

The virus had mutated again. It had not become radically different. People who had gotten sick in the second wave had a fair amount of immunity to another attack, just as people sickened in the first wave had fared better than others in the second wave. But it mutated enough to rekindle the epidemic. Some places were not touched by the third wave at all. But many—in fact, most—were.

By any standard except that of the second wave, this third wave was a lethal epidemic. And in a few isolated areas—such as Michigan—December and January were actually worse than October. In Phoenix, for three days in a row in mid-January the new cases set a record exceeding any in the fall. The city of Quitman, Georgia, issued twenty-seven epidemic ordinances that took effect December 13, 1918, after the disease had seemingly passed. In Savannah, Georgia, on January 15 theaters and public gathering places were ordered closed—for a third time—with even more rigid restrictions than before. San Francisco had gotten off lightly in the fall wave, as had the rest of the West Coast, but the third wave struck hard.

In fact, of all the major cities in the country, San Francisco had confronted the fall wave most honestly and efficiently. On October 22, the mayor, the public health director, the Red Cross, the Chamber of Commerce, and the Labor Council jointly declared in a full-page newspaper ad, WEAR A MASK AND SAVE YOUR LIFE!, claiming that it was "99 percent proof against influenza."[11] By October 26, the Red Cross had distributed one hundred thousand masks. Simultaneously, while local facilities geared up to produce vaccines, thousands of doses of a vaccine were raced across the continent on the country's fastest train.

In San Francisco, people felt a sense of control. Instead of the paralyzing fear found in too many other communities, San

Francisco seemed to offer inspiration. When schools closed, teachers volunteered as nurses, orderlies, and telephone operators. On November 21, every siren in the city signaled that masks could come off. San Francisco had—to that point—survived with far fewer deaths than had been feared, and its citizens believed that the masks deserved the credit. But if anything helped, it would have been the organization the city's public health director, William Hassler, had set in place in advance.

The people of San Francisco thought that *they* had controlled it, that *they* had stopped it. They were mistaken. The masks, hanging loose about the face and made of only a few layers of gauze, were not much good. The city had simply been lucky. Two weeks later, the third wave struck. Although at its peak it killed only half as many as did the second wave, it made the final death rates for the city the worst on the West Coast.

With the exception of a few small outposts that isolated themselves, by early 1919 there was only one place the virus seemed to have missed.

Australia had been hit by the mild first wave but had escaped the lethal variant that caused the second wave. It had escaped because of a strict quarantine of incoming ships. The quarantine kept the virus out, and kept the continent safe, until late December 1918 when, with influenza having receded around the world, a troopship carrying ninety ill soldiers arrived. Although they, too, were quarantined, the disease penetrated—apparently through medical personnel treating the troops.

By then the strain had lost much of its lethality. In Australia the death rate from influenza was far less than in any other Westernized nation on earth, barely one-third that of the United States, not even one-quarter that of Italy. But it was lethal enough.

The pandemic itself—even in this, its most mild incarnation in the developed world—was terrifying enough that those who lived through it as children remembered it not as influenza at all, but as plague.

And the virus was still not finished. All through the spring of 1919 a kind of rolling storm moved above the earth, intermittent, unleashing sometimes a sudden localized shower, sometimes even a lightning bolt, and sometimes passing over with only a rumble of threatened violence in the distant and dark sky.

It remained violent enough to do one more thing.

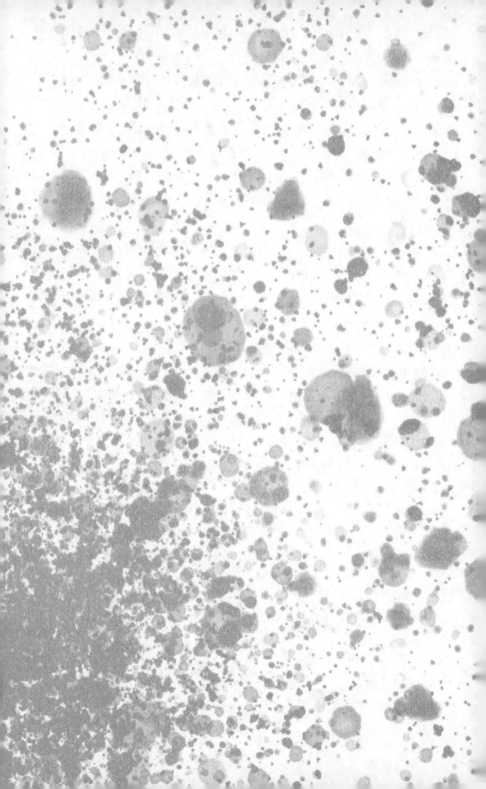

PART V

—— ✚ ——

AFTER 1918

CHAPTER FIFTEEN

~~~

A President's Health

The Great War ended on November 11, 1918. The Allied powers—which included the United States, Great Britain, France, and Russia—were victorious.

Now two million American troops were returning from Europe. One out of every sixty-seven soldiers in the army had died of influenza; however, Army Surgeon General William Gorgas had largely triumphed over every other disease. US soldiers almost entirely escaped malaria, for example, even while it struck down tens of thousands of French, British, and Italian soldiers. One of Gorgas's last acts was to try to prevent these troops from carrying diseases back home. Soldiers were kept isolated for seven days before they boarded ships returning to the US and were deloused before embarking. Soldiers would be bringing no disease home.

+

The overwhelming majority of the virus's victims, especially in the Western world, recovered quickly and fully. This was, after all, only influenza.

But it sometimes caused one final complication. The influenza virus affected the brain and nervous system. All high fevers cause delirium, but this was something else. The connection between influenza and various mental instabilities seemed clear. The evidence was almost entirely anecdotal, the worst and weakest kind of evidence, but it convinced the vast majority of contemporary observers that influenza could alter mental processes. It seemed to affect the brain.

Observers also linked influenza to an increase in Parkinson's disease a decade after the pandemic. Many believed that the virus could cause schizophrenia. In 1927 the American Medical Association's review of hundreds of medical journal articles from around the world concluded, "There seems to be general agreement that influenza may act on the brain . . . There is no doubt that the neuropsychiatric effects of influenza are profound and varied . . . The effect of the influenza virus on the nervous system is hardly second to its effect on the respiratory tract."[1] In 1934 a similar comprehensive review by British scientists agreed: "There would appear to be no doubt that influenza exerts a profound influence on the nervous system."[2]

Many victims suffered problems for months and years, in the equivalent of what we call "long COVID."

Months after supposedly recovering from his illness, the great poet Robert Frost wondered, "What bones are they that rub together so unpleasantly in the middle of you in extreme emaciation . . . Here it is as late as this (1919 A.D.) and I don't know whether or not I'm strong enough to write a letter yet."[3]

Cincinnati health commissioner William H. Peters told the American Public Health Association almost a year after the epidemic that "phrases like 'I'm not feeling right,' 'I don't have my usual pep,' 'I'm all in since I had the flu' have become commonplace." Cincinnati's public health agencies had examined 7,058 influenza victims since the epidemic had ended and found 5,264 needed some medical assistance. Of those examined, 643 had heart problems, and an extraordinary number of prominent citizens who'd had influenza had died suddenly early in 1919. While it was hardly a scientific sample, Peters believed that few victims had escaped without some physical changes caused by influenza.

Either the virus or the immune response or both could destroy brain cells, make it difficult to concentrate, alter behavior, or interfere with thinking. Even if this occurred in only a minority of cases, the virus's impact on the mind was nonetheless real. And that impact would, by terrible coincidence, have a profound effect indeed.

✚

In January 1919, Kansas congressman William Borland died while in France, the third congressman to be killed by the virus. That same month, also in Paris, "Colonel" Edward House, Wilson's close confidant, collapsed with influenza for a third time.

House had gotten influenza during the first wave in March 1918. He was confined to his home for two weeks, then went to Washington and relapsed. He spent three weeks in bed at the White House. Although the spring version of the virus often provided immunity to future waves, House was struck down a second time in November 1918. He got up for the first time in ten days on November 30 and met with French prime minister Georges Clemenceau for fifteen minutes. Afterward, House noted, "Today is the first day I have taken up my official work in person for over a week. I have had influenza ten days and have been exceeding[ly] miserable . . . So many have died since this epidemic has scourged the world. Many of my staff have died."[4]

Now, in January 1919, the virus attacked him for a third time. He was sick enough that some newspapers reported him dead. House wryly called the obituaries "all too generous."[5] But the blow to his health was heavy; more than a month after his supposed recovery, he wrote in his diary, "When I fell sick in January I lost the thread of affairs and I am not sure that I have ever gotten fully back."[6]

There were affairs of some magnitude to attend to in Paris in early 1919. Representatives of various nations had come there to set the terms of peace after the war. Several thousand men from dozens of countries circled around the edges of decision-making. Germany would play no role in these decisions; Germany would simply be dictated to. A council of ten of the most powerful nations supposedly determined the agenda. Even within this tight circle was a tighter one, the "Big Four"—the United States,

France, Britain, and Italy. In reality, only three of those four nations mattered. Indeed, only three men mattered: France's prime minister Georges Clemenceau, known as "the Tiger"; Great Britain's prime minister David Lloyd George; and US president Woodrow Wilson, who arrived in Europe the most popular political figure in the world.

A year earlier, in 1918, Wilson had presented his fourteen-point plan for war aims and peace terms in a speech before Congress. It was essentially a blueprint for how he believed world peace might be achieved, and he planned to follow it as terms of peace were decided in Paris. He would face stiff opposition from Clemenceau.

For weeks and then months, their meetings dragged on. Wilson, Clemenceau, and Lloyd George were themselves doing much of the actual negotiating. They were bargaining and wheedling, they were demanding and insisting, and they were rejecting.

Often only five or six men would be in a room, including translators. Often, even when Clemenceau and Lloyd George had others present, Wilson represented the United States alone, with no staff, no secretary of state, no one else. Discussions were seemingly endless. But they were deciding the future of the world.

+

In the month of February 1919, deaths in Paris from influenza and pneumonia climbed back up to 2,676, more than half the peak death toll. Wilson's daughter Margaret had influenza in Belgium in February; in March Wilson's wife, Edith; her secretary, chief White

House usher Irwin Hoover; and Cary Grayson, Wilson's personal White House physician and perhaps the single man Wilson trusted the most, were all ill. Clemenceau and Lloyd George both seemed to have mild cases of influenza, too.

Meanwhile the sessions with Lloyd George and Clemenceau were often brutal. In late March, Wilson told his wife, "Well, thank God I can still fight, and I'll win." On March 29, he said, "M. Clemenceau called me pro-German and left the room."

On April 3, a Thursday, at 3 p.m., Wilson seemed in fine health, according to Grayson, the White House physician. Then, at 6 p.m., Grayson saw Wilson "seized with violent paroxysms of coughing, which were so severe and frequent that it interfered with his breathing."

The attack came so suddenly that Grayson suspected that Wilson had been poisoned, that an assassination attempt had been made. But it soon became obvious the diagnosis was simpler, if only marginally more reassuring.

Joseph Tumulty, Wilson's chief of staff, had stayed in Washington to monitor political developments at home. He and Grayson exchanged telegrams daily, sometimes several times a day. The information of the president's illness was too sensitive for a telegram, but Grayson did wire him, "The President took very severe cold last night; confined to bed."[7] Simultaneously he wrote a confidential letter to be hand-delivered: "The President was taken violently sick last Thursday. He had a fever of over 103 and profuse diarrhea . . . [It was] the beginning of an attack of influenza. That night was one of the worst through which I have ever passed. I was able to control the spasms of coughing, but his condition looked very serious."[8]

Donald Frary, a young aide on the American peace delegation in Paris, came down with influenza the same day Wilson did. Four days later, he died at age twenty-five.

For several days Wilson lay in bed, unable to move. On the fourth day, he sat up. Grayson wired Tumulty, "Am taking every precaution with him . . . Your aid and presence were never needed more."[9]

Meanwhile the negotiations continued; Wilson, unable to participate, was forced to rely on Colonel House as his stand-in. Just before getting sick, Wilson had threatened to leave the peace process and return to the United States without a treaty rather than yield on his principles. For several days Wilson continued to talk about leaving France, telling his wife, "If I have lost the fight, which I would not have done had I been on my feet, I will retire in good order, so we will go home."[10]

Then, on April 8, Wilson insisted upon personally rejoining the negotiations. Too ill to go out, Grayson wrote that the president "insisted upon holding conferences while he was still confined to his sickbed."[11] Clemenceau and Lloyd George came to his bedroom, but the conversations did not go well. His public threat to leave had infuriated Clemenceau.

The people surrounding Wilson began to take note of changes in him. A member of the Secret Service noticed that Wilson "lacked his old quickness of grasp, and tired easily"[12] and that he became obsessed with details such as who was using the official automobiles.

White House chief usher Irwin Hoover recalled several new and very strange ideas that Wilson suddenly believed, including one that his home was filled with French spies: "Nothing we could say could disabuse his mind of this thought. About this time he also acquired a peculiar notion he was personally responsible for all the property in the furnished place he was occupying . . . Coming from the president, whom we all knew so well, these were very funny things, and we could but surmise that something queer was happening in his mind. One thing was certain: he was never the same after this little spell of sickness."[13]

Grayson confided to Tumulty, "This is a matter that worries me."[14]

Then, abruptly, still on his sickbed, only a few days after he had threatened to return to the United States unless Clemenceau yielded to his demands, without warning to or discussion with any other Americans, Wilson suddenly abandoned the principles he had previously insisted upon. He yielded to Clemenceau everything of significance Clemenceau wanted, virtually all of which Wilson had earlier opposed. Even Lloyd George commented on Wilson's "nervous and spiritual breakdown in the middle of the conference."[15]

Grayson wrote, "These are terrible days for the president physically and otherwise."[16]

✚

Less than six months later, in October 1919, Wilson suffered a major and debilitating stroke. For months, First Lady Edith Wilson and Grayson would control all access to him and function as arguably the most important policy makers in the country.

It is of course impossible to say what Wilson would have done had he not become sick. Perhaps he would have made the concessions to Clemenceau anyway. Or perhaps he would have sailed home as he had threatened to do just as he was succumbing to the disease. Then either there would have been no treaty, or his walkout would have forced Clemenceau to compromise.

No one can know what would have happened. We can only know what did happen.

Influenza did visit the peace conference. Influenza did strike Wilson. Influenza did weaken him physically, and—precisely at the most crucial point of negotiations—influenza did at the least drain from him stamina and the ability to concentrate. That much is certain. And it is almost certain that influenza affected his mind in other, deeper ways.

Historians agree with virtual unanimity that the harshness of the Paris peace treaty toward Germany—forcing Germany to accept all responsibility for starting the war and imposing enormous reparations upon Germany—helped create the economic hardship, nationalistic reaction, and political chaos that fostered the rise of Adolf Hitler.

It did not require hindsight to see the dangers of this treaty. They were obvious at the time. The influential economist John Maynard Keynes quit Paris calling Wilson "the greatest fraud on earth." Later he wrote, "We are at the dead season of our fortunes . . . Never in the lifetime of men now living has the universal element in the soul of man burnt so dimly."[17]

Herbert Hoover, who served as an adviser to the United States delegation in Paris and was a decade away from becoming the thirty-first president of the United States, believed the treaty would tear down all Europe and said so.

Soon after Wilson made his concessions, a group of young American diplomatic aides and advisers met in disgust to decide whether to resign in protest. The group was made up of men who would become among the most influential people in the country, including two secretaries of state. Several did decide to resign, and one, Adolf Berle Jr., later an assistant secretary of state, wrote Wilson a blistering letter of resignation: "I am sorry that you did not fight our fight to the finish and that you had so little faith in the millions of men, like myself, in every nation who had faith in you. Our government has consented now to deliver the suffering peoples of the world to new oppressions, subjections, and dismemberments—a new century of war."[18]

Wilson had influenza, only influenza.

CHAPTER SIXTEEN

❧

Viral Legacy

Virtually all accounts of the 1918 pandemic speak of three waves. Contemporaries viewed it that way, but that's simply because they, like many people two years into COVID-19, simply got tired of it. Almost no place closed schools or took any other public health precautions in 1920. Yet, in truth, there was a fourth wave.

On September 20, 1919, many of the best scientists in the country met to try to reach a consensus on the cause of influenza or the best course of treatment for it. They were unable to agree, but *The New York Times* stated that the conference marked the beginning of a joint federal, state, and city effort to prevent a recurrence.

By February 7, 1920, influenza had returned with enough ferocity that the Red Cross declared, "Owing to the rapid spread of influenza, the safety of the country demands, as a patriotic duty, that all available nurses or anyone with experience in nursing communicate with the nearest Red Cross chapters or special local epidemic committees, offering their services."[i]

The year 1920 would see either the second or third most deaths from influenza and pneumonia in the twentieth century (sources differ). In eight weeks in early 1920, eleven thousand influenza-related deaths occurred in just New York City and Chicago, and in New York City more cases would be reported on a single day than on any one day in 1918. Several cities—Detroit, Milwaukee, and others—recorded more deaths in 1920 than in any previous wave.

Only in 1921 did influenza deaths return to prepandemic levels; only then did influenza finally fade into the background in both the United States and the world. It did not disappear. It continued to attack, but with far less power, partly because the virus mutated and new variants behaved like most influenza viruses, partly because people's immune systems adjusted. But it left a legacy.

Some of that legacy was positive. Around the world, authorities made plans for international cooperation on health, and the experience led to restructuring of public health efforts throughout the United States. The New Mexico Department of Public Health was created; Philadelphia rewrote its city charter to reorganize its public health department; from Manchester, Connecticut, to Memphis, Tennessee, and beyond, emergency hospitals were transformed into permanent ones. And the pandemic motivated Louisiana senator Joe Ransdell to begin pushing for the establishment of the National Institutes of Health, although he did not win his fight until a far milder influenza epidemic in 1928 reminded Congress of the events of a decade earlier.

But the loss of life was by far the greater legacy.

Even before the epidemic ended, New York City Health Department head Royal Copeland estimated that twenty-one thousand children in the city had been made orphans by the epidemic. The number of children who lost only one parent was far higher.

There were other aftershocks impossible to quantify. The world was still sick, sick to the heart. The war itself . . . The senseless deaths at home, on top of all else . . . Wilson's betrayal of his principles when he gave in to Clemenceau, a betrayal that penetrated the soul . . . The utter failure of science in the face of the disease . . .

✛

Nearly all those who lived through the 1918 pandemic are dead now. Now the memory lives in the minds of those who only heard stories, who heard how their mother lost her father, how an uncle became an orphan, or heard an aunt say, "It was the only time I ever saw my father cry." Memory dies with people.

The novelists of the 1920s who had lived through it had little to say about it. Ernest Hemingway, William Faulkner, and F. Scott Fitzgerald said next to nothing of it. Katherine Anne Porter was ill enough that her obituary was prepared for printing. She recovered. Her fiancé did not. Her haunting novella of the disease and the time, *Pale Horse, Pale Rider*, is one of the best—and one of the few—sources for what life was like during the disease. And she lived through it in Denver, a city that, compared to those on the East Coast, was struck only a glancing blow.

Historians who examine epidemics and analyze how societies respond to them have generally argued that those with power blamed the poor for their own suffering and sometimes tried to stigmatize and isolate them. Those in power, they have observed, often tried to keep safe by imposing order, which gave them some feeling of control, some feeling that the world still made sense.

Yet the 1918 influenza pandemic did not in general demonstrate a preference of race or class. There was a correlation between population density—and hence class—and deaths, but the disease still struck down everyone. The deaths of soldiers of such promise and youth particularly hit home with everyone. The disease was universal.

During the second wave, many local governments collapsed, and those who held the real power in a community—such as Philadelphia's wealthy citizens—took over. Generally they strove to protect the entire community rather than to split it, to distribute resources widely rather than to guarantee resources for themselves. Despite that effort, though, censorship and outright lies in the press and by government leaders endangered communities because they destroyed trust.

It is impossible to quantify how many deaths the lies caused. It is impossible to quantify how many young men died because the army refused to follow the advice of its own surgeon general. But while those in authority were reassuring people that this was influenza, only influenza, at least some people must have believed them, at least some people must have exposed themselves to the virus in ways they would not have otherwise, and at least some of these people must have died who would otherwise have lived. And fear really did kill people. It killed them because those who feared would not care for many of those who needed but could not find care, those who needed only hydration, food, and rest to survive.

It is also impossible to state with any accuracy the death toll. The statistics are estimates only, and one can only say that the totals are numbing.

The few places in the world that then kept reliable vital statistics under normal circumstances could not keep pace with the disease. In the United States, only large cities and twenty-four states kept accurate enough statistics for the US Public Health Service to include them in their database. Even in those places, everyone—from physicians to city clerks—was trying to survive or help others survive. Record keeping had low priority, and in the aftermath little effort was made to compile accurate numbers. Many who died never saw a doctor or nurse. Outside the developed world, the situation was far worse, and in the rural regions of India, Russia (which was engaged in a brutal civil war), China, Africa, and South America, where the disease was often strongest, good records were all but nonexistent.

The first significant attempt to quantify the death toll came in 1927. An AMA-sponsored study estimated that twenty-one million died. When today's media refers to a death toll of "more than twenty million" in stories on the 1918 pandemic, the source is this study.

In the 1940s Macfarlane Burnet, the Nobel laureate who spent most of his scientific life studying influenza, estimated the death toll at fifty to one hundred million. This figure is likely more accurate.

The world's population in 1918 was approximately 1.8 billion. If 100 million people died, that would mean that in two years— and with most of the deaths coming in a horrendous twelve weeks in the fall of 1918—more than 5 percent of the people in the world died from influenza.

Today's world population is 8 billion. To give a sense of the impact in today's world of the 1918 pandemic, one has to adjust for population. If one uses the AMA's lowest estimate of deaths—the 21 million figure—that means a comparable figure today would be nearly 90 million dead. The higher estimates translate into between 225 and 450 million dead. Those numbers are not meant to terrify—although they do. Medicine has advanced since 1918 and would have considerable impact on the mortality rate. Those numbers are meant simply to communicate what living through the pandemic was like.

Yet even those numbers understate the horror of the disease. In a normal influenza epidemic, 10 percent or fewer of the deaths fall among those aged between sixteen and forty. In 1918 that age group, the men and women with most vitality, most to live for, most of a future, accounted for more than half the death toll, and within that group the worst mortality figures fell upon those aged twenty-one to thirty.

The Western world suffered the least, not because its medicine was so advanced but because urbanization had previously exposed its population to influenza viruses, so many people already had some immunity. In the United States, around 0.65 percent of the total population died, with roughly double that percentage of young adults killed. Of developed countries, Italy suffered the worst, losing approximately 1 percent of its total population. Russia may have suffered more, but few numbers are available for it.

The virus simply ravaged the less developed world. In Mexico, the most conservative estimate of the death toll is 2.3 percent of the entire population, and other reasonable estimates put the death toll over 4 percent. That means somewhere between 5 and 9 percent of all young adults died.

And in the entire world, although no one will ever know with certainty, it seems more than just possible that 5 percent—and in the less developed countries approaching 10 percent—of the world's young adults were killed by the virus.

CHAPTER SEVENTEEN

~~~

Investigating Answers

By the start of World War I, the revolution in American medicine led by William Welch had triumphed. That revolution had radically transformed American medicine, forcing its teaching, research, art, and practice through the filter of science.

Those in the United States capable of doing good scientific research remained a small, almost tiny, group. It could be counted in the dozens. They all knew each other, all had shared experiences, and nearly all had at least some connection to the Hopkins, the Rockefeller Institute, Harvard, and a handful of other elite universities.

The bonds that held these scientists together were not bonds of friendship. Some of them had no love for each other, many had happily embarrassed a rival by finding flaws in their work, and they had no illusions about one another's virtues.

Yet they all also recognized that whatever each other's flaws might be, each of them had strengths, remarkable strengths. Their work was good enough that even if in error, one could often find in that error something new, something important, something to build upon. It was an exclusive group that included very few women. In bacteriology these very few women did not extend far beyond Anna Williams and Martha Wollstein. (The leading female medical scientist in the United States of that era, Florence Sabin, was not a bacteriologist, and hence is not a part of this story. Sabin was the first woman to graduate from the Hopkins medical school, the first woman full professor at any medical school in the country—at the Hopkins—and the first woman elected to the National Academy of Sciences.)

All of these scientists had worked frenetically in their laboratories from the first days of the disease, and none of them had stopped. In those most desperate of circumstances, the most desperate circumstances in which they—and arguably any scientist—ever worked, most of them had willingly, hopefully, accepted less evidence than they would normally have to reach a conclusion. But for all their frenzy of activity, they had still avoided chaos; they had always proceeded from well-grounded hypotheses.

They also recognized their failures. They had entered the first decades of the twentieth century confident that science, even if its victories remained limited, would triumph. Now Victor Vaughan, the dean of the University of Michigan's medical school who'd worked alongside Welch and others inspecting army camps, told a colleague, "Never again allow me to say that medical science is on the verge of conquering disease."

But they had not quit. Now this scientific fellowship was beginning its hunt for answers about influenza. It would take longer than they knew.

So far each laboratory had been working in isolation, barely communicating with the others. Investigators had to meet, to trade ideas and new laboratory techniques, to discuss findings not yet published or that one investigator thought unimportant that might mean something to another. They had to try to piece together some way to make concrete progress against this disease. They had to sift through the mess of their failures for clues to success.

On October 30, 1918, with the epidemic on the East Coast fading to manageable proportions, Hermann Biggs, a bacteriologist and former student of Welch's, organized an influenza commission of leading scientists. Cole, Park, and Lewis were included among the commission of epidemiologists and pathologists. Welch, still recovering from influenza in Atlantic City, was too ill to attend. Biggs opened the first meeting by echoing Vaughan: "[T]here has never been anything which compares with this in importance . . . in which we were so helpless."[1]

But unlike Vaughan he was angry. They had seen the epidemic coming for months. Yet public health officials and scientists had done nothing to prepare. "We ought to have been able to obtain all the scientific information available now or that can be had six months from now before this reached us at all." Biggs was determined that they would now address this problem and solve it.

It would not be so easy. And even in that first meeting the problems presented themselves. They still knew next to nothing about this disease. They could not even agree upon its nature. The pathology was too confusing. The symptoms were too confusing.

Even this late, Cole still wondered whether it was influenza at all.

They reached no consensus about the disease and moved on to discuss the likely pathogen. There, too, they could reach not even a tentative conclusion.

They knew so little. So little. They knew only that isolation worked. The New York State Training School for Girls had quarantined itself, even requiring people delivering supplies to leave them outside. It had had no cases. The Trudeau Sanatorium in upstate New York had similar rules. It had no cases. Across the continent, a naval facility in San Francisco on an island enforced rigid quarantine. It had no cases. But the investigators had no proof for why the isolation worked.

Yet the commission ended with agreement. They agreed on lines of approach, on the work that needed to be done. Only on that—in effect, on how little they knew—could they agree.

They intended to proceed down two paths: one exploring the epidemiology of the disease, the other tracing clues in the laboratory.

The epidemiological studies would have the added benefit of exciting and transforming another emerging field of medicine. In November 1918 the American Public Health Association created the Committee on Statistical Study of the Influenza Epidemic. One committee member called this "an opportunity to show what statistics, especially vital statistics, and its methods can do for preventive medicine."[2] Two months later, in January 1919, leaders of the army, navy, and Public Health Service joined with the Census Bureau to form an influenza committee that grew into a permanent statistical office.

Meanwhile, the most massive scientific inquiry ever under-taken was coming together. Biggs's commission met three more times. At every meeting of every medical specialty, of every public health organization, in every issue of every medical journal, influenza dominated the agenda. In Europe it was the same.

Every major laboratory in the United States continued to focus on the disease. Lewis in Philadelphia kept after it, as did others at the University of Pennsylvania, as well as a team of Harvard researchers in Boston.

At the Rockefeller Institute, Cole put "every available man" to work on it—as well as Martha Wollstein. When Captain Francis Blake, who had been part of the army's pneumonia commission, visited his old colleagues at the institute at Christmas, he found everyone "working tooth and nail on this influenza business with monkeys and everything else." A week later, out of the army and back at Rockefeller, Blake said, "I shall be so glad when we can get all this business off our hands and finished up and I can do something else for a change, as it seems as though I have done nothing but work on, and eat, and dream about and live with pneumonia and influenza for six months."[3]

He would not be free of it any time soon.

Slowly, over a period of months, a body of knowledge began to form. Investigators began to learn about the firestorm that had roared around the world and was continuing to smolder.

First, they confirmed what they had suspected: the lethal fall disease was a second wave of the same disease that had hit in the spring. They based their conclusion on the fact that those exposed to the spring wave had substantial immunity to the later one.

Statistics also confirmed what every physician, indeed every person, already knew. In the civilian population as well, young adults had died at extraordinary, and frightening, rates. The elderly, normally the group most susceptible to influenza, not only survived attacks of the disease but were attacked far less often. This resistance of the elderly was a worldwide phenomenon. The most likely explanation is that an earlier pandemic, one so mild as to not attract attention, resembled the 1918 virus closely enough that it provided immunity to this older generation.

Finally, a door-to-door survey in several cities also confirmed the obvious: people living in the most crowded conditions suffered more than those with the most space. It also seemed—although this was not scientifically established—that those who went to bed the earliest after becoming ill, stayed there the longest, and had the best care also survived at the highest rates. Those findings meant of course that the poor died in larger numbers than the rich. Questions about race and the epidemic, however, yielded contradictory information: African Americans seemed to have lower morbidity—they got sick at lower rates—but higher case mortality.

In the laboratory, however, answers continued to be out of reach. The pathogen remained unknown. Enormous resources were poured into this research everywhere. Yet all this work had not solved the mystery. The problem did not lie in any lack of clues. The problem lay in distinguishing the few clues that led in the right direction from all those that led in the wrong direction.

As the second wave of influenza had broken upon the world, thousands of scientists had attacked the problem. In Germany and France they had attacked it, in Britain and Italy, in Australia and Brazil, in Japan and China. But as 1919 wore away, then 1920, as the disease drifted toward mildness, one at a time these scientists began to peel off. They found the problem too difficult. Or the techniques seemed too inadequate to address it, or it lay too far from their old interests or knowledge base. After two years of extraordinary—and continuing—efforts by many of the world's best investigators, in 1920 Welch made a frustrating prediction: "I think that this epidemic is likely to pass away and we are no more familiar with the control of the disease than we were in the epidemic of 1889. It is humiliating, but true."[4]

+

The greatest questions remained the simplest ones: What caused influenza? What was the pathogen? Was Pfeiffer right when he identified a cause and named it *Bacillus influenzae*? And if he was not right, then what did cause it? What was the killer?

The pursuit of this question is a classic case of how one does science, of how one finds an answer, of the complexity of nature, of how one builds a solid scientific structure.

All through the epidemic, bacteriologists had mixed results looking for *Bacillus influenzae*. People as skilled as Park and Williams, Lewis, and Avery had all been unable to isolate it from the first cases they studied. Then they adjusted their techniques, changed the medium in which they grew it, added blood heated to a particular temperature to the medium, changed the dyes used for staining, and they found it.

Park and Williams soon found it so consistently that Park assured the National Research Council it was the cause of the disease. The Public Health Service believed it to be the cause. Lewis, despite initial misgivings, thought it the cause.

At Rockefeller, Martha Wollstein had studied *Bacillus influenzae* since 1905. In the midst of the pandemic, she had become convinced it did cause the disease. She had been so confident that the vaccine she prepared included *only Bacillus influenzae.* Her work convinced her Rockefeller colleagues as well; they all took her vaccine, even though they were among the few in the country with access to another Rockefeller vaccine that had proven itself effective.

Midway through the pandemic, failure to find *Bacillus influenzae* seemed a mark not of good science but of incompetence. At the same time, Avery published the new techniques he had developed that made it much easier to grow the organism. Bacteriologists began to find what they were looking for. In camp after camp, bacteriologists fell into line. Bacteriologists at Camp MacArthur in Texas were not alone in their determination "to obtain the highest possible incidence of B. influenzae," and they found it in 88 percent of lungs. But they did so not through any irrefutable laboratory tests; they simply looked through a microscope and identified the bacteria by appearance. Such observations are subjective and not proof, only indications.

Civilian investigators isolated *Bacillus influenzae* with similar regularity. Yet even with all the findings of it, the picture remained confusing. For rarely was it found alone. And sometimes it was still not being found at all. In some cases even the most experienced investigators found the bacillus rarely. These reports created increasing doubt about *Bacillus influenzae*. Scientists did not doubt the word of those who found it. They did not doubt that the bacillus could cause disease and kill. But they began to doubt what finding it proved.

There were other questions. In the midst of the epidemic, under the greatest pressures, many bacteriologists had compromised the quality of their work in the hope of getting quick results.

Park and Williams had been among the first to proclaim *Bacillus influenzae* the likely cause of the epidemic. In mid-October, Park still held to that position. They had prepared and distributed a vaccine based largely upon their conviction.

But even Park and Williams had made compromises. Now, as the epidemic waned, they continued their investigations with great deliberateness. They had always been best at testing hypotheses, looking for flaws, improving upon and expanding others' more original work. Now, chiefly to learn more about the organism in the hope of perfecting a vaccine and serum—but also to test their own hypothesis that *Bacillus influenzae* caused influenza— they started an extensive series of experiments.

For a decade, scientists had tried to make a vaccine and antiserum for *Bacillus influenzae*. No one had succeeded. Park and

Williams believed they now understood why. As they explored it further, they became more and more convinced that *Bacillus influenzae*, similar to pneumococcus, included dozens of strains. And each strain was different enough that an immune serum that worked against one would not work against the others. In fact, Williams found "ten different strains in ten different cases."[5]

In early 1919, Park and Williams reversed their position. The *Bacillus influenzae*, they now said, did not cause influenza. They stated, "This evidence of multiple strains seems to be absolutely against the influenza bacillus being the cause of the pandemic. It appears to us impossible that we should miss the epidemic strain in so many cases while obtaining some other strain so abundantly. The influenza bacilli, like the streptococci and pneumococci, are in all probability merely very important secondary invaders."[6] This was a significant change in thinking.

Many others were beginning to change their thinking on the matter, too. But the subject remained controversial. What it came down to was that nearly all investigators believed their own work. If they had found the influenza bacillus in abundance, they believed it caused influenza. If they had not found it, they believed it did not cause influenza.

Only a very few saw beyond their own work and were willing to change their minds—and contradict their previous findings— as Park and Williams were. In doing so they demonstrated an extraordinary openness, an extraordinary willingness to look with a fresh eye at their own experimental results.

But after they convinced themselves—and many others—that

the influenza bacillus did not cause influenza, they moved on. They stopped working on influenza, partly because they were convinced they were right, partly because the New York City municipal laboratory was losing the funding to do true research, and partly because they were getting old.

Through the 1920s, investigators continued to work on the problem. For years it was, as Nobel laureate Macfarlane Burnet said, the single most important question in medical science.

In England, Alexander Fleming had, like Avery, concentrated on developing a medium in which the bacillus could flourish. In 1928 he left a petri dish uncovered with staphylococcus bacteria growing in it. Two days later he discovered a mold that inhibited the growth. He extracted from the mold the substance that stopped the bacteria and called it "penicillin." Fleming found that penicillin killed many types of bacteria, including staphylococcus, hemolytic streptococcus, pneumococcus, gonococcus, and diphtheria bacilli—yet it did no harm to the influenza bacillus. He did not try to develop penicillin into a medicine. He said he simply used penicillin "for the isolation of influenza bacilli."[7] (Fleming never did see penicillin as an antibiotic. But a decade later Howard Florey and Ernst Boris Chain, funded by the Rockefeller Foundation, did. They developed Fleming's observation into the first wonder drug, an antibiotic that is commonly used to treat bacterial infections including strep throat. In 1945, Florey, Chain, and Fleming shared the Nobel Prize.)

In 1929 at a major conference on influenza, Welch gave his personal assessment: "Personally I do feel there is very little evidence that [*Bacillus influenzae*] can be the cause . . . The fact has always appealed to me that influenza is possibly an infection due to an unknown virus."[8] But in 1931 Pfeiffer himself still argued that the pathogen he had called *Bacillus influenzae* and that informally bore his name was the most likely cause.

That same year, Richard Shope seemed to prove Pfeiffer wrong. Shope was a protégé of Paul Lewis, who had died tragically in Brazil of yellow fever while he was trying to develop a vaccine for it. Now Shope published three papers in a single issue of the *Journal of Experimental Medicine*. His work appeared in good company. In that same issue were articles by Avery; by Thomas Rivers, who in 1926 defined the difference between bacteria and viruses and who has been called "the father of American virology"; and by Karl Landsteiner, who had just won the Nobel Prize. All of these scientists were at the Rockefeller Institute. Each of Shope's articles was about influenza. He honored Lewis by listing him as the lead author on one.

Lewis had found the cause of influenza, at least in swine. It was a virus. We now know that the virus Lewis found in swine descended directly from the 1918 virus. It is still unclear whether humans gave the virus to swine, or swine gave it to humans (although it seems more likely that humans gave it to swine). By the time Lewis did this work with pigs, the virus had mutated into mild form, or the pigs' immune systems had adjusted to it, or both, since the virus alone seemed to cause only mild disease. Shope's work demonstrated that with *Bacillus influenzae* as a secondary invader the virus could still be highly lethal.

Shope's work was momentous and provocative. Two years later in 1933, three British scientists, Wilson Smith, Christopher Andrewes, and Patrick Laidlaw, built on his work: at last, they found the human pathogen. It was a virus like Shope's swine influenza. Their discovery helped answer the key question of what caused influenza in humans, something scientists had been working toward since the onset of the pandemic in 1918.

AFTERWORD

This is the fifth afterword I have written for this book.

In January 2020, before a single case of COVID-19 had been identified in the United States, I wrote an opinion piece with the working title "This Virus Cannot Be Contained," which eventually ran in *The Washington Post*. Now, as I write this nearly three years later, the United States has exceeded 1 million deaths from COVID-19 while worldwide deaths are estimated at 20 million—and counting. For weeks the country set a new record each day for COVID-19 hospitalizations, with deaths breaching 5,000 a day and cases reaching 1.35 million a day. The US situation was among the worst anywhere at the time. But the virus was also surging worldwide, even in those countries that once seemed to have it under control. It began resurfacing in China, New Zealand, and Taiwan, demonstrating how relentless it is. We cannot relax against it, ever.

But that does not mean that there is nothing we can do to defend ourselves against this virus, or against inevitable future pandemics. I have been asked over and over what lessons from 1918 might apply. I have the same answer now that I gave in the original afterword of this book and in each update since: leaders in a society must not lose the public's trust. The way to do that is to tell the truth. A leader must make whatever horror exists concrete. Only then will people be able to break it apart.

That was the first lesson. The second, proven again in 2020, is that public health measures—the nonpharmaceutical interventions (NPIs) of social distancing, proper ventilation, masks, handwashing, and so forth—*work*.

Those two lessons are intertwined. Public health measures work only if people use them and sustain that use, but in a free society that happens only when leadership tells people the truth and convinces them to cooperate. Since COVID-19 surfaced, the leadership of some nations did tell the truth. Others did not. What leaps out from the evidence is that national death rates were much lower where the lessons of 1918 were consistently applied from the beginning, and much higher where they were not.

✚

Both the 1918 influenza virus and SARS-CoV-2—the virus causing the disease known as COVID-19—transmit exactly the same way. Both viruses are expelled when shouting, talking, or even breathing, either in droplets, which fall to the ground fairly quickly, or smaller and lighter aerosolized packets of virus, which can float in the air for hours like dust motes. Both viruses primarily attack the respiratory system. Both can bind to cells in the nose, mouth, and throat—the upper respiratory tract—which makes them highly transmissible. Both can also bind to cells deep in the lungs—the lower respiratory tract—which can cause viral pneumonia and make them lethal. Both viruses commonly cause such symptoms as dry cough, body aches, headache, diarrhea, and fever. Both viruses can kill.

In addition, though both viruses primarily attack the respiratory system, the 1918 influenza virus and SARS-CoV-2 can infect virtually every organ in the body, and they have especially serious neurological and cardiovascular impacts. Both viruses cause illness that can linger for extended periods. The 1918 virus was linked to problems that didn't surface for several years. It is too soon to know how long-lasting COVID-19 damage can be.

The final similarity: both viruses mutate. Influenza actually does so at a faster rate, yet SARS-CoV-2 obviously mutates rapidly enough to beset the world with variant after variant. If, when, and to what extent it will stabilize are unknown as I write this.

The 1918 virus and SARS-CoV-2 also have important differences. Of course they differ in molecular structure, in the mechanism by which they bind to cells, and in many other highly technical ways. But they also differ in very important ways that one does not need knowledge of molecular biology to observe.

First, the 1918 virus was much more lethal. Most modern epidemiologists have concluded that Macfarlane Burnet, the Nobel laureate who studied influenza, was right when he estimated that it killed between 50 and 100 million people; adjusted for population, that would equal somewhere between 225 and 450 million people today. The most dire worst-case projections for COVID-19 do not call for anything like those numbers. At this writing, COVID-19 has infected most of the world's population and has killed—officially—almost 7 million people; the real death toll is perhaps 20 million.

Although less dangerous, COVID-19 is significantly more transmissible than either ordinary influenza or the 1918 virus.

Another important difference is that the 1918 virus primarily killed children under ten and otherwise healthy young adults. Seasonal influenza also attacks children, but not like the 1918 virus. In 1918 children under the age of ten died at a rate roughly twenty times greater than the number of children that age who die today. With COVID-19, it's the opposite; the overwhelming majority of deaths occur in people older than sixty-five. In 1918 well over 90 percent of the excess deaths occurred in people younger than sixty-five.

Also, someone who is infected with influenza but has no symptoms or does not yet show symptoms can transmit the virus, but only for a relatively brief time period, as short as a few hours to at most not much more than a day. This accounts for about 30 percent of transmission. In COVID-19, the period when someone does not yet have symptoms but can transmit it can last two days. People who never develop any symptoms at all can transmit the disease for an even longer period, though it's not yet known precisely how long. A study by the CDC found that 59 percent of cases come from people who do not have symptoms at the time—24 percent from people who never develop symptoms, 35 percent from those who later develop symptoms. This is why mask use by the public matters for COVID-19; isolating once you feel sick is too late.

The viruses also differ in the fourth dimension—time. The 1918 pandemic moved through any given community usually in six to eight weeks; closure orders rarely lasted more than four weeks. When it was gone, it seemed to disappear, and although subsequent waves did return, only the second wave struck hard everywhere in the world. While the 1918 pandemic was much more intense and killed many more people, COVID-19 has caused much more severe and much longer lasting economic damage, and in many ways it has caused more stress, as many schools and businesses were closed for months on end.

Finally, unlike with COVID, and despite the fact that the public was lied to in 1918, no segment of the public in 1918 dismissed the pandemic as inconsequential. Deaths were too common, and they came too fast for anyone to think it anything but a deadly, serious event. That was not the case with COVID-19. In my view, there is no comparison between resistance to public health measures in 2020 and in 1918. With death everywhere in 1918, people accepted virtually every measure that might help. Some resistance did develop in cities where measures were lifted and then reimposed, but it was not politicized; it bore no resemblance to the widespread opposition we have seen with COVID-19, which clearly has been politicized.

✚

About the time the first edition of this book was published, in 2004, President George W. Bush had already increased funding for biodefense. So-called "bird flu," the H5N1 virus, was then threatening the world with a pandemic that could have rivaled or exceeded 1918 in lethality. President Bush read the book and made pandemic preparedness a priority of his administration. Because of my knowledge of 1918, I was asked to participate in the initial meetings to recommend public health measures that might mitigate the damage of a pandemic. In those meetings, I repeatedly pushed the need for the truth. Everyone from the public health community always agreed, although occasionally a politician would protest, "You don't want to scare people." I or someone else would reply, "In fact you do, when there's a reason to be scared." The federal plan that emerged—and every state and territorial plan, which are all modeled on it—emphasized that communication to the public had the highest priority and honesty was the key to that priority.

Participants in those meetings were also unanimous that no politician—not the president, not a cabinet secretary, possibly not even the head of the CDC—should be the spokesperson, because no matter how popular that person was, some portion of the population would distrust them. We all believed a scientist should do most of the communicating. Anthony Fauci, then head of the National Institute of Allergy and Infectious Diseases, did not participate in those meetings, but we were unanimous that if a pandemic occurred while he still served, he would be the best person for the role.

Much of the discussions centered on nonpharmaceutical

interventions, or NPIs, things to do when you don't have any drugs—social distancing, ventilation, closings, handwashing, and so on. I supported NPIs in principle, but based on 1918 data, I had some skepticism. My concern was compliance.

The army's experience in the 1918 influenza pandemic was instructive. Of 120 large army camps in the United States, 99 imposed some kind of social distancing, including some very extreme and aggressive actions; 21 took no action whatsoever. Yet there was zero statistical difference between camps that did and did not employ these measures. The epidemiologist who did the study found that the only significant differences were in how well camps *enforced* the measures. Generally enforcement grew lax over a period of weeks, so the measures had no effect, while NPIs did have an impact in camps "where they were rigidly carried out." Yet so few camps did it right that statistics showed no difference.

How should we interpret this? On the one hand, if an army camp in the middle of a war failed to exercise enough discipline to execute orders that saved lives, what prospect was there that civilians during peacetime would? On the other, the overcrowded barracks of a World War I training camp made it much harder to contain a disease than in even the most densely populated civilian community, which gave some reason for optimism that NPIs could work—*if* people complied.

It was a matter of discipline, a matter of, as football coaches say, execution. And, as in football, execution depended on attention to detail and motivation. So we were back to the importance of communication. NPIs work well only when people comply, and 2020 proved that.

Some people in 2020, before vaccines became available, supported the idea of pursuing herd immunity through natural infection. Once enough people acquired natural immunity, the argument went, the outbreak would die out with minimal economic impact. But pursuing herd immunity through natural infection would have made no sense for multiple reasons.

First, COVID-19 is at least ten times as deadly as the influenza virus that circulates every year. The death toll could have been even more horrific than it has been.

Second, real-world experience made it clear that upwards of two-thirds of the population would have to be infected with the virus—before any mutations—to achieve herd immunity. Death toll aside, the *lowest* estimate of how many people will develop long COVID exceeds ten million in the United States and probably runs into several tens of millions. We still have no idea of what those consequences will be for them; complications range from fatigue to far more severe neurological and cardiovascular problems. Whether this damage will cut years off survivors' lives or simply affect their quality of life is unknown. Had the government followed the herd immunity approach, it would have exposed hundreds of millions of people to this unknown risk; that made, and still makes, little sense.

Sweden publicly denied pursuing the "herd immunity" policy but came close to employing it in reality. The results? The best comparison is with neighboring Scandinavian countries, which have similar demographics, culture, and physical environment. Sweden has triple the per capita death toll of Denmark, six times that of Finland, and eight times that of Norway, all of which were much more aggressive in lockdowns, masks, and other NPIs. These deaths did not buy better economic performance. Sweden is dead center with its neighbors on their economies.

As I write this, roughly 70 percent of the entire population has been vaccinated against COVID-19. Approximately 95 percent of the entire US population has been infected or vaccinated or both. So virtually the entire population has at least some protection against this severe disease. In addition, evidence strongly suggests that vaccines provide better protection than natural infection alone. As a result, we have returned to something like a prepandemic normal, but the virus will continue to infect people. It has become endemic and will never disappear. The 1918 virus mutated its way into seasonal influenza. The most optimistic view is that COVID-19 could become much like the common cold, but it is nowhere near that yet—it is still killing at a rate nearly triple the deadliest year ever for ordinary seasonal influenza and ten times a mild year for influenza.

✚

For fifteen years, I gave talks on preparedness and said there was one question we didn't know the answer to. In 1918 doctors and nurses knew they would face infectious disease on a routine basis, and they accepted that risk. But doctors and nurses today don't regularly encounter infectious disease. Would health-care workers risk their lives in a modern pandemic? Now we know the answer. They have been called heroes. They are.

One of the most positive things to come out of this recent pandemic was the way in which scientists around the world rose to the occasion. There has been an explosion of collaboration and communication, which has led to extraordinary and rapid progress. Some of that will likely continue. All of us will be better for it.

We need to remember what many countries around the world have demonstrated: even in the absence of vaccines, other measures can control the virus. NPIs work. In order of importance, they are social distancing, masks, ventilation (it disturbs me that this very important aspect never got the emphasis it should have), and handwashing (which matters, though less than thought initially).

The likelihood of pandemics is increasing. Pathogens have always been able to infect humans, but if this occurred in an isolated region, the disease might die out before ever getting the chance to spread to the outside world. Today hardly any part of the world is that remote. In addition, humans are now moving deeper and deeper into previously remote regions, where they provide animal pathogens with more chances to spill over into humans. As the natural hosts of the pathogens disappear due to deforestation, these pathogens are ever more likely to jump species into humans.

When a new pathogen emerges, no matter how far vaccine technology advances, it will still take many months to produce and distribute an adequate supply. So we'd better put the lessons we've learned to use, and we'd better do more to prepare. What have we learned? The first two items on the list are the lessons from 1918, which COVID-19 has confirmed:

Number one, tell the truth. Trust matters, and truth is key to trust. A study of 177 countries found that the system of government—whether they were autocratic, democratic, or communist—had much less to do with death tolls than whether people trusted institutions and trusted each other. Nations ranking high on those two measures did well; those ranking low, including the US, did not.

Number two, NPIs work.

Those two lessons are obviously connected. Without the truth, the public will not cooperate, and NPIs will not have the impact they could have. Telling the truth includes saying we don't know everything at the beginning.

COVID-19 demonstrated the need for flexibility. A best practice for one disease may not be a best practice for another. Disinfecting surfaces and handwashing matter relatively little for COVID-19 but could be hugely important for something else. And we must also address much larger, systemic issues as well, issues that require action at the international, national, state, and local levels.

The International Health Regulations, a legally binding treaty signed by nearly every country in the world, were revised after the first SARS outbreak to improve the worldwide response. But the regulations need a major revision again, starting with dramatically improving the early warning system for any emerging disease. This failed in the COVID-19 pandemic.

The International Society for Infectious Diseases runs its own separate and informal system called the Program for Monitoring Emerging Diseases (ProMED), which monitors all sources of information, including social media. On December 30, 2019, ProMED provided the first notice to anyone outside China of COVID-19, but the virus had already been infecting people for at least six weeks before even this informal warning came. The World Health Organization (WHO) and CDC both initiated their response to COVID-19 based on this informal ProMED report, and official word still lagged behind it. The system of notification must be expanded and improved dramatically, and it must be independent of national governments—governments tend to be overly cautious even in the rare instances when they share information promptly.

And when WHO does act, it needs to act more decisively, starting with its messaging. On January 30, 2020, at least three weeks after COVID-19 had reached several other countries, it declared a "public health emergency of international concern." That language marks WHO's highest level of alert, but it purposely avoided the word *pandemic*, partly for bureaucratic reasons—outside of influenza, the term had no legal meaning and did not trigger any additional actions—and partly for fear it would cause overreaction. Many governments took virtually no action until WHO did begin using *pandemic* a month later.

On the national level—and on the state and local levels in the

United States—governments and the private sector must become more *inefficient*. Yes, it's inefficient for a government to stockpile personal protective equipment like masks, or ventilators, or anti-viral drugs, especially if they expire or require maintenance. It's inefficient for a hospital to do the same. It's inefficient for state and local governments to support their public health infrastructure. It's also inefficient to have a functioning fire department—until you have a fire.

Before the pandemic, countries around the world were rated on how prepared they were. The United States ranked first because of its extensive planning for a pandemic, its exercising of those plans, and its resources. COVID-19 demonstrated that planning does not equal preparation. Nor do resources equal preparation. COVID-19 demonstrated once again how much leadership matters. A response to any crisis will always come down to leadership. No matter how good a plan, how good the preparation, someone has to execute the plan. The plan starts with the truth.

Thus we end this afterword where we began, and where the other afterwords in previous editions of this book ended: The final lesson of 1918, a simple one yet most difficult to execute, is that those who occupy positions of authority must retain the public's trust. The way to do that is to distort nothing, to put the best face on nothing, to try to manipulate no one.

TIMELINE OF KEY EVENTS

1863: International Committee of the Red Cross is founded in Switzerland as a nongovernmental institution to aid victims of war, violence, and disease.

1876: Johns Hopkins University opens in Baltimore, Maryland.

1881: Clara Barton founds the American arm of the Red Cross.

1884: Dr. William Henry Welch begins teaching at Johns Hopkins.

1893: Johns Hopkins University opens America's first modern medical school.

1903: The Rockefeller Institute for Medical Research establishes its own laboratory in New York City.

March 4, 1913: Woodrow Wilson takes office as the United States' twenty-eighth president.

July 28, 1914: World War I begins in Europe.

April 2, 1917: The United States enters World War I.

April 13, 1917: President Wilson creates the Committee on Public Information to encourage public support for the war.

August 1917: The US Army opens Camp Devens in Massachusetts to train soldiers.

March 1918: First known outbreaks of unusual influenza at Camp Funston in Kansas.

Early April 1918: First unusual outbreaks of influenza activity in Europe occur in Brest, France.

April 10, 1918: First appearance of influenza in the French army.

Late April 1918: Influenza reaches Paris and Italy.

May 1918: Influenza reaches Spain and earns the name "Spanish Influenza" or "Spanish flu."

Late May 1918: Influenza reaches Mumbai (then called Bombay) and Shanghai.

June 1918: British troops returning from mainland Europe bring influenza to England.

June 30, 1918: The British freighter City of Exeter docks at Philadelphia. Crew members are very sick and die of pneumonia, but quarantine keeps it from spreading to civilians.

July 1918: Influenza reaches Denmark and Norway.

August 8, 1918: US colonel Charles Hagadorn takes command of the army's Camp Grant.

August 10, 1918: Death rates from influenza begin soaring among French sailors stationed at Brest.

September 1918: Influenza reaches New Zealand.

September 4, 1918: Influenza spreads to military personnel in New Orleans.

September 7, 1918: The first case of influenza is found at Camp Devens. Soldiers spread influenza from Boston to Philadelphia.

September 15, 1918: New York City's first death from influenza occurs.

September 21, 1918: The first death from influenza in Washington, DC, occurs.

September 28, 1918: Philadelphia's Liberty loan parade takes place, resulting in significant spread of influenza.

October 3, 1918: Wilmer Krusen bans all public meetings in Philadelphia.

Mid to late October 1918: First influenza vaccines are distributed, but they protect against the wrong pathogen and offer no protection against the influenza virus.

November 11, 1918: World War I officially ends.

April 3, 1919: President Wilson contracts influenza while in France negotiating terms of peace and becomes disoriented.

October 1919: Wilson suffers a debilitating stroke, very possibly a complication of his earlier influenza attack.

Early 1920: The fourth wave of the pandemic occurs.

1921: Influenza deaths return to prepandemic levels.

1926: Thomas Rivers defines the difference between viruses and bacteria.

1931: Richard Shope publishes three major articles about influenza in the *Journal of Experimental Medicine*.

1933: Three British scientists identify the virus that causes influenza in humans.

January 10, 2020: The World Health Organization announces that the outbreak of a pneumonia-like illness first reported in China in December 2019 is caused by the 2019 Novel Coronavirus, also known as COVID-19.

KEY FIGURES

Oswald Avery: Scientific researcher who investigated pneumococcus bacteria, revolutionizing biological sciences.

Rupert Blue: Surgeon general and head of the US Public Health Service in 1918.

Frank Macfarlane Burnet: Nobel laureate who spent most of his scientific career studying influenza.

Joe Capps: Chief of service at the hospital at Camp Grant in 1918.

Georges Clemenceau: Prime minister of France from 1906 to 1909 and again from 1917 to 1920. He clashed with President Wilson during negotiations for the Treaty of Versailles.

Rufus Cole: First director of the Rockefeller Institute Hospital.

George Creel: Journalist and prominent supporter of President Wilson who led the Committee on Public Information.

Jane Delano: Founder of the American Red Cross nursing service.

David Lloyd George: Prime minister of the United Kingdom from 1916 to 1922, he was a key part of negotiations for the Treaty of Versailles.

William Crawford Gorgas: Surgeon general of the United States Army from 1914 to 1918, he was in charge of medicine and health in the military.

Charles Hagadorn: US Army colonel who commanded Camp Grant.

"Colonel" Edward House: Close confidant of President Wilson.

Wilmer Krusen: Philadelphia's public health director in 1918.

Paul Lewis: Scientific researcher who attempted to develop an influenza vaccine based on isolating and killing pneumococci. He also discovered the virus that causes influenza in swine.

Elizabeth Martin: Head of the Pennsylvania state chapter Council of National Defense's Women's Division and Emergency Aid.

William Park: Scientific researcher at New York City's Department of Public Health who led the attempt to develop an influenza vaccine in 1918.

Richard Pfeiffer: German scientist who first isolated *Bacillus influenzae*, which he believed to cause influenza.

Richard Shope: Scientific researcher who published groundbreaking research on influenza in the 1930s.

Victor Vaughan: Dean of the University of Michigan's medical school who worked alongside William Welch inspecting army camps during World War I.

William Henry Welch: Scientist who revolutionized American medicine and helped lead attempts to prevent infectious diseases in American military camps during World War I.

Anna Williams: Scientific researcher at New York City's Department of Public Health who led the attempt to develop an influenza vaccine in 1918.

Woodrow Wilson: The twenty-eighth president of the United States, from 1913 to 1921, who presided over the country's participation in World War I.

Martha Wollstein: Bacteriologist who studied Pfeiffer's bacillus at Rockefeller Institute as early as 1905 and who worked to create an influenza vaccine during the pandemic.

ENDNOTES

Part I: Before

Chapter One: A Revolution from Nothing

1. "There was a strong demand": Benjamin Gilman, quoted in Flexner, *American Saga*, 125.

Chapter Two: The Modernization of American Medicine

1. "The prestige and knowledge . . . ": Welch to father, March 21, 1876, Welch Papers at JHU.

2. "I feel as if . . . ": Welch to stepmother, March 26, 1877, Welch Papers at JHU.

3. "I cannot make much . . .": Quoted in Flexner and Flexner, *William Henry Welch,* 112.

4. "I sometimes feel rather . . . ": Quoted in Flexner and Flexner, *William Henry Welch,* 112.

5. "the power to transform . . . ": Ludmerer, *Learning to Heal*, 128.

6. "Not to turn to you . . . ": Flexner and Flexner, *William Henry Welch*, 263.

7. "without redeeming features . . . ": Ludmerer, *Learning to Heal*, 169–73.

8. "that the hospital laboratory . . .": Benison, *Tom Rivers*, 68.

Part II: The US Army and Influenza

Chapter Four: America Goes to War

1. "To fight you must . . . ": Walworth, *Woodrow Wilson*, v. 2, 97.

2. "It isn't an army we must . . . ": Stephen Vaughn, *Holding Fast the Inner Lines: Democracy, Nationalism, and the Committee on Public Information* (1980), 3.

3. "Truth and falsehood are arbitrary . . .": Vaughn, *Holding Fast the Inner Lines,* 3.

4. "one white-hot mass . . .": Vaughn, *Holding Fast the Inner Lines*, 3.

5. "Inscribed in our banner . . .": Vaughn, *Holding Fast the Inner Lines*, 141.

6. "I am Public Opinion": Vaughn, *Holding Fast the Inner Lines*, 169.

7. "every printed bullet . . . ": Murray, *Red Scare*, 12.

8. "an important element . . .": Vaughn, *Holding Fast the Inner Lines*, 126.

9. "questionable jokes and other . . . ": *Philadelphia Inquirer,* Sept. 1, 1918.

10. "ninety percent of . . . ": Kennedy, *Over Here*, 54.

11. "who spreads pessimistic . . . ": Vaughn, *Holding Fast the Inner Lines*, 155.

12. "exert itself in any . . . ": Red Cross news release, Aug. 23, 1917, entry 12, RG 52, National Archives.

13. "so that one may . . . ": Aug. 24, 1917 memo, entry 12, RG 52, National Archives.

14. "Confectioners and restaurants . . . ": See, for example, the *Arizona Gazette*, Sept. 26, 1918.

15. "if this plan were . . . ": Lavinia Dock, et al., *History of American Red Cross Nursing* (1922), 958.

Chapter Five: Keeping the Troops Healthy

1. "prevention of infectious disease": Flexner to Vaughan, June 2, 1917, Flexner papers.

2. "Although pneumonia occurs . . . ": Rufus Cole, et al., "Acute Lobar Pneumonia Prevention

and Serum, Treatment," Monograph of the Rockefeller Institute for Medical Research 7 (Oct. 1917), 4.

3. "in view of the . . . ": See, for example, Gorgas to Commanding Officer, Base Hospital, Camp Greene, Oct. 26, 1917, entry 29, file 710, RG 112, National Archives.

4. "detention camps for . . . ": Welch diary, Dec. 28, 1917, Welch Papers at JHU.

Chapter Six: Unusual Outbreak

1. "At the end of May . . . ": Quoted in Jordan, *Epidemic Influenza*, 78.

2. "It swept over the . . . ": Jordan, *Epidemic Influenza*, 85.

3. "of very short duration . . . ": T. R. Little, C. J. Garofalo, and P. A. Williams, "B Influenzae and Present Epidemic," *The Lancet* (July 13, 1918), quoted in *JAMA* 71, no. 8 (Aug. 24, 1918), 689.

4. "has completely disappeared": Letter from London of Aug. 20, 1918, quoted in *JAMA* 71, no. 12 (Sept. 21, 1918), 990.

Chapter Seven: Lethal Waves

1. "The opinion was reached . . . ": Soper, "Influenza Pandemic in the Camps."

2. "grossly overcrowded": Crosby, *America's Forgotten Pandemic*, 38.

3. "The mess officer . . . ": Major R. C. Hoskins, "Report of Inspection on Sept. 30, 1918," Oct. 9, 1918, RG 112, National Archives.

4. "were looked upon . . . ": Major Paul Wooley, "Epidemiological Report on Influenza and Pneumonia, Camp Devens, August 28 to October 1, 1918," entry 29, RG 112, National Archives.

5. "Stated briefly . . . ": Major Paul Wooley, "Epidemiological Report on Influenza and Pneumonia, Camp Devens, August 28 to October 1, 1918," entry 29, RG 112, National Archives.

6. "These men start . . . ": Dr. Roy N. Grist to "Burt," *British Medical Journal* (Dec. 22–29, 1979).

7. "You will proceed . . . ": Victor Vaughan, *A Doctor's Memories* (1926), 431.

8. "This must be . . . ": Cole to Flexner, May 26, 1936, file 26, box 163, Welch Papers at JHU.

9. "It is important that . . . ": "Memo for Camp and Division Surgeons," Sept. 24, 1918, entry 710, RG 112, National Archives.

10. "New men will almost . . ." and "urgent military necessities": Brigadier General Richard to adjutant general, Sept. 25, 1918, entry 710, RG 112, NA; see also Charles Richard to chief of staff, Sept. 26, 1918, entry 710, RG 112, National Archives.

Part III: Fear

Chapter Eight: A Model City

1. "sway the ideas of whole . . . ": Quoted in Victoria De Grazia, "The Selling of America, Bush Style," *The New York Times* (Aug. 25, 2002).

2. "Call the bluff . . . ": Gregg Wolper, "The Origins of Public Diplomacy: Woodrow Wilson, George Creel, and the Committee on Public Information" (1991), 80.

Chapter Nine: Camp Grant

1. "capable and energetic" and "of course an excellent . . . ": Frederick Russell and Rufus Cole, Camp Grant inspection diary, June 15–16, 1918, Welch Papers at JHU.

2. "different type of pneumonia . . . ": Welch to Dr. Christian Herter, treasurer, Rockefeller Institute for Medical Research, Jan. 13, 1902, Welch Papers at JHU.

3. "a great thing . . . ": Richard Pearce to Major Joseph Capps, July 10, 1918, Camp Grant, influenza files, National Academy of Sciences Archives.

4. "This is a very important . . . ": Rufus Cole to Richard Pearce, July 24, 1918, influenza files, National Academy of Sciences Archives.

5. "a routine measure" and "one of the most . . . ": Joseph Capps, "Measures for the Prevention and Control of Respiratory Disease," *JAMA* (Aug. 10, 1918), 448.

6. "Until further notice . . . ": Quoted in Kovinsky, report to SG, Nov. 5, 1918, entry 29, RG 112, National Archives.

7. "There must as a military . . . ": Charles Hagadorn, Sept. 20, 1918, entry 29, box 383, RG 112, National Archives.

8. "to mingle in any . . . ": Kovinsky, report to Surgeon General William Gorgas, Nov. 5, 1918.

9. "except under extraordinary circumstances": "Bulletin of the Base Hospital," Oct. 3 and Oct. 4, 1918, RG 112, National Archives.

10. "very carefully controlled": Stone to Warren Longcope, July 30, 1918, entry 29, RG 112, National Archives.

11. "to the closest hospital . . . ": Selma Epp, transcript of unaired interview for "Influenza 1918," *American Experience*, Feb. 28, 1997.

12. "Don't get frightened": *Philadelphia Public Ledger*, Oct. 8, 1918.

13. "People were dying . . . ": Oral history of Clifford Adams, June 3, 1982, provided by Charles Hardy of West Chester University.

Chapter Ten: Only Influenza

1. "In nonfatal cases . . .": Maj. General Merritt W. Ireland, ed., *Medical Department of the United States Army in the World War*, v. 9, *Communicable Diseases* (1928), 159.

2. "those seen in acute . . . ": Ireland, *Communicable Diseases*, 149.

3. "unusual in other viral . . . ": Edwin D. Kilbourne, MD, *Influenza* (1987), 202.

4. "marked hyperemia" and "the brain tissues . . . ": Douglas Symmers, MD, "Pathologic Similarity Between Pneumonia of Bubonic Plague and of Pandemic Influenza," *JAMA* (Nov. 2, 1918), 1482.

5. "occurred in nearly . . . ": Ireland, *Communicable Diseases*, 160.

6. "I could not have . . . ": Comments at USPHS conference on influenza, Jan. 10, 1929, file 11, box 116, Welch Papers at JHU.

Chapter Eleven: *Bacillus Influenzae*

1. "astonishing numbers": Quoted in David Thomson and Robert Thomson, *Annals of the Pickett-Thomson Research Laboratory*, v. 9, *Influenza* (1934), 265.

2. "Will your lab undertake . . .": Pearce wire to Park, Sept. 18, 1918, influenza files, National Academy of Sciences Archives.

3. "Will undertake work": Park wire to Pearce, Sept. 19, 1918, influenza files, National Academy of Sciences Archives.

4. "We had plenty of . . . ": Diary, undated, chap. 22, p. 23, Williams papers.

5. "The only results so . . . ": Park to Pearce, Sept. 23, 1918, National Academy of Sciences Archives.

6. "would seem to be . . . ": Park to Pearce, Sept. 26, 1918, National Academy of Sciences Archives.

7. "small and bare . . . ": Dubos, *The Professor, the Institute, and DNA* (1976), 78.

8. "His attitude had . . . ": Dubos, *Professor*, 173.

Part IV: Deadly Decisions

Chapter Twelve: Confronting the Virus

1. "Owing to disordered . . .": Cole to Pearce, July 19, 1918, National Academy of Sciences Archives.

2. "*Surgeon General's Advice to Avoid Influenza*": *Washington Evening Star*, Sept. 22, 1918.

3. "The work at National . . . ": Lavinia Dock, et al., *History of American Red Cross Nursing* (1922), 969.

Chapter Thirteen: Desperation

1. "Your committee has no . . . ": Mrs. J. Willis Martin to Mayor Thomas Smith, Oct. 8, 1918, Council of National Defense papers, Historical Society of Philadelphia.

2. "The death toll for . . . ": Undated memo, entries 13B–D2, RG 62, National Archives.

3. "the death rate for . . . ": Krusen to Navy Surgeon General William Braisted, Oct. 6, 1918, entry 12, RG 52, National Archives.

4. "They stopped people . . . ": Clifford Adams, Charles Hardy oral history tapes.

5. "all persons with two hands": Unidentified newspaper clipping in epidemic scrapbook, Oct. 9, 1918, College of Physicians Library, Philadelphia.

6. "The fear in the hearts . . . ": Susanna Turner, transcript of unaired interview for "Influenza 1918," *American Experience*, Feb. 27, 1997.

7. "The first casualty when . . . ": Many citations of this comment originally made in 1917, including *Newsday*, June 15, 2003.

8. *"There is no cause . . . "*: *Washington Evening Star*, Oct. 13, 1918.

9. "Even if there was . . . ": Susanna Turner, transcript of unaired interview for "Influenza 1918," *American Experience*, Feb. 27, 1997.

10. "It kept people apart . . . ": William Sardo, transcript of unaired interview for "Influenza 1918," *American Experience*, Feb. 27, 1997.

11. "There wasn't much visiting . . . ": Patricia J. Fanning, "Disease and the Politics of Community: Norwood and the Great Flu Epidemic of 1918" (1995), 139–42.

Chapter Fourteen: Failed Efforts

1. "urgent call on . . . ": See, for example, *JAMA* 71, no. 17 (Oct. 26, 1918): 1412, 1413.

2. "The results have been . . ." and "In the four cases . . . ": F. B. Bogardus, "Influenza Pneumonia Treated by Blood Transfusion," *New York Medical Journal* (May 3, 1919), 765.

3. "One way to keep . . . ": *Arizona Gazette*, Nov. 26, 1918.

4. "had been tested sufficiently . . .": Numerous papers both in and outside New York City, see, for example, *Philadelphia Public Ledger*, Oct. 18, 1918.

5. "the statistical evidence . . . ": George Whipple, "Current Comment, Vaccines in Influenza," *JAMA* (Oct. 19, 1918), 1317.

6. "The value of vaccination . . . ": E. A. Fennel, "Prophylactic Inoculation against Pneumonia," *JAMA* (Dec. 28, 1918), 2119.

7. "Unfortunately we as yet have . . . ": Editorial, *JAMA* 71, no. 17, (Oct. 26, 1918), 1408.

8. "Nothing should be done . . . ": Editorial, *JAMA* 71, no. 19 (Nov. 9, 1918), 1583.

9. "If the epidemic continues . . . ": Collier, *Plague of the Spanish Lady*, 266.

10. "In the later stages . . . ": Edwin O. Jordan, *Epidemic Influenza* (1927), 355–56.

11. "Wear a mask and . . .": June Osborn, ed., *Influenza in America, 1918–1976: History, Science, and Politics* (1977), 11.

Part V: After 1918

Chapter Fifteen: A President's Health

1. "There seems to be general . . . ": Jordan, *Epidemic Influenza*, 278–80.

2. "There would appear to be . . . ": Thomson and Thomson, *Influenza*, v. 10, 768.

3. "What bones are they . . . ": Dorothy Ann Pettit, "A Cruel Wind: America Experiences the Pandemic of Influenza, 1918–1920, A Social History" (1976), 173.

4. "Today is the first day . . . ": Diaries, House collection, Nov. 30, 1918, quoted in Pettit, "Cruel Wind," 186.

5. "all too generous.": *New York Telegram*, Jan. 14, 1919, quoted in Pettit, "Cruel Wind," 186.

6. "When I fell sick . . . ": Quoted in Arthur Walworth, *Woodrow Wilson*, v. 2 (1965), 279.

7. "The President took very severe . . . ": Grayson wire to Tumulty, 8:58 a.m., April 4, 1919, box 44, Tumulty papers, Library of Congress.

8. "The President was taken . . . ": Grayson to Tumulty, April 10, 1919, marked PERSONAL AND CONFIDENTIAL, box 44, Tumulty papers.

9. "Am taking every precaution . . . ": Grayson to Tumulty, 11:00 a.m., April 8, 1919, box 44, Tumulty papers.

10. "If I have lost . . . ": Edith Wilson, *My Memoir* (1939), 249, quoted in Crosby, *America's Forgotten Pandemic*, 191.

11. "insisted upon holding . . . ": Cary Grayson, *Woodrow Wilson: An Intimate Memoir* (1960), 85.

12. "lacked his old quickness . . .": Hugh L'Etang, *The Pathology of Leadership* (1970), 49.

13. "Nothing we could say . . . ": Irwin H. Hoover, *Forty-two Years in the White House* (1934), 98.

14. "This is a matter that . . . ": Grayson to Tumulty, April 10, 1919, box 44, Tumulty papers.

15. "nervous and spiritual . . .": Lloyd George, *Memoirs of the Peace Conference* (1939), quoted in Crosby, *America's Forgotten Epidemic*, 193.

16. "These are terrible days . . .": Grayson to Tumulty, April 30, 1919, box 44, Tumulty papers.

17. "We are at the dead . . . ": John Maynard Keynes, *Economic Consequences of the Peace* (1920), 297.

18. "I am sorry that . . . ": "Papers Relating to the Foreign Relations of the United States, The Paris Peace Conference" (1942–1947), 570–74, quoted in Schlesinger, *The Age of Roosevelt*, v. 1, *Crisis of the Old Order 1919–1933* (1957), 14.

Chapter Sixteen: Viral Legacy

1. "Owing to the rapid . . . ": Memo to division managers from chairman of influenza committee, Feb. 7, 1920, RG 200, National Archives.

Chapter Seventeen: Investigating Answers

1. "[T]here has never been . . . ": Transcript of Influenza Commission minutes, Oct. 30, 1918, Winslow papers.

2. "an opportunity to . . . ": presented at American Public Health Association meeting, Dec. 11, 1918, entry 10, file 1622, RG 90, National Archives.

3. "every available man," "working tooth and. . . ," and "I shall be so glad . . . ": Quoted in Petit, "Cruel Wind," 229.

4. "I think that this epidemic . . . ": Comments by Welch on influenza bacillus paper, undated, file 17, box 109, Welch Papers at JHU.

5. "ten different strains . . . ": Park comments, transcript of Influenza Commission minutes, Dec. 20, 1918, Winslow papers.

6. "This evidence of multiple . . . ": Thomson and Thomson, *Influenza*, v. 9, 498.

7. "for the isolation of . . . ": Thomson and Thomson, *Influenza*, v. 9, 287, 291, 497.

8. "Personally I do . . . ": Welch comments, USPHS Conference on Influenza, Jan. 10, 1929, box 116, file 11, Welch Papers at JHU. Conference itself reported in *Public Health Reports* 44, no. 122.

SELECTED BIBLIOGRAPHY

Archives and Collections

Alan Mason Chesney Archives, Johns Hopkins University
William Welch papers

American Philosophical Society
Simon Flexner Papers

College of Physicians, Philadelphia
Influenza papers

Historical Society of Philadelphia
Council of National Defense papers

Library of Congress
Joseph Tumulty papers

National Academy of Sciences
Biographical files for Oswald Avery, Rufus Cole, Alphonse Dochez, Eugene Opie,
Thomas Rivers, Hans Zinsser
Committee on Medicine and Hygiene 1918 files
Committee on Psychology/Propaganda Projects file
Executive Committee of Medicine 1916–1917 files
Influenza files
Medicine and Related Sciences, 1918 Activities Summary

National Archives
Red Cross records
US Army Surgeon General records
US Navy Surgeon General records
US Public Health Service records

Schlesinger Library, Radcliffe College
    Anna Wessel Williams papers

Sterling Library, Yale University
    Charles-Edward Winslow papers

Newspapers

Arizona Gazette

Newsday

Philadelphia Inquirer

Philadelphia Public Ledger

Washington Evening Star

Articles and Transcripts

Bogardus, F. B. "Influenza Pneumonia Treated by Blood Transfusion." *New York Medical Journal* 109, no. 18 (May 3, 1919): 765–68.

Capps, Joe. "Measures for the Prevention and Control of Respiratory Disease." *JAMA* 71, no. 6 (Aug. 10, 1918): 571–73.

Cole, Rufus, et al. "Acute Lobar Pneumonia Prevention and Serum Treatment." Monograph of the Rockefeller Institute for Medical Research 7 (Oct. 1917).

de Grazia, Victoria. "The Selling of America, Bush Style." *New York Times*, Aug. 25, 2002.

Epp, Selma. Transcript of unaired interview for "Influenza 1918," *American Experience*, Feb. 28, 1997.

Fennel, E. A. "Prophylactic Inoculation against Pneumonia." *JAMA* 71, no. 26, (Dec. 28, 1918): 2115–18.

Grist, N. R. "Pandemic Influenza 1918." *British Medical Journal* 2, no. 6205 (Dec. 22–29, 1979): 1632–33.

Little, T. R., C. J. Garofalo, and P. A. Williams, "B Influenzae and Present Epidemic," *The Lancet* (July 13, 1918), quoted in *JAMA* 71, no. 8 (Aug. 24, 1918).

Sardo, William. Transcript of unaired interview for "Influenza 1918," *American Experience*, Feb. 28, 1997.

Soper, George, MD. "The Influenza-Pneumonia Pandemic in the American Army Camps, September and October 1918." *Science*, Nov. 8, 1918.

Symmers, Douglas, MD. "Pathologic Similarity Between Pneumonia of Bubonic Plague and of Pandemic Influenza." *JAMA* 71, no. 18 (Nov. 2, 1918): 1482–83.

Whipple, George. "Current Comment, Vaccines in Influenza." *JAMA* 71, no. 16 (Oct. 19, 1918).

Books

Benison, Saul. *Tom Rivers: Reflections on a Life in Medicine and Science: An Oral History Memoir.* Cambridge, Mass.: MIT Press, 1967.

Collier, R. *The Plague of the Spanish Lady: The Influenza Pandemic of 1918–1919.* New York: Atheneum, 1974.

Crosby, Alfred W. *America's Forgotten Pandemic: The Influenza of 1918.* Cambridge, England, and New York: Cambridge University Press, 1989.

Dock, Lavinia, et al. *History of American Red Cross Nursing.* New York: Macmillan, 1922.

Dubos, René. *The Professor, the Institute, and DNA.* New York: Rockefeller University Press, 1976.

Flexner, James Thomas. *An American Saga: The Story of Helen Thomas and Simon Flexner.* Boston: Little, Brown, 1984.

Flexner, Simon, and James Thomas Flexner. *William Henry Welch and the Heroic Age of American Medicine.* New York: Viking, 1941.

Grayson, Cary. *Woodrow Wilson: An Intimate Memoir.* New York: Holt, Rinehart, & Winston, 1960.

Hoover, Irwin H. *Forty-two Years in the White House.* New York: Houghton Mifflin, 1934.

Ireland, Merritt W., ed. *Medical Department of the United States Army in the World War,* v. 9, *Communicable Diseases.* Washington, D.C.: U.S. Army, 1928.

Jordan, Edwin O. *Epidemic Influenza.* Chicago: American Medical Association, 1927.

Kennedy, David. *Over Here: The First World War and American Society.* New York: Oxford University Press, 1980.

Keynes, John Maynard. *Economic Consequences of the Peace.* New York: Harcourt, Brace and Howe, 1920.

Kilbourne, E. D., MD. *Influenza.* New York: Plenum Medical, 1987.

L'Etang, Hugh. *The Pathology of Leadership.* New York: Hawthorn Books, 1970.

Ludmerer, Kenneth M. *Learning to Heal: The Development of American Medical Education.* New York: Basic Books, 1985.

Murray, Robert. *Red Scare: A Study in National Hysteria.* Minneapolis: University of Minnesota Press, 1955.

Osborn, June E. *Influenza in America, 1918–1976: History, Science and Politics.* New York: Prodist, 1977.

Schlesinger, Arthur. *The Age of Roosevelt,* v. 1, *Crisis of the Old Order 1919–1933.* Boston: Houghton Mifflin, 1957.

Thomson, David, and Robert Thomson. *Annals of the Pickett-Thomson Research Laboratory,* vols. 9 and 10, *Influenza,* Baltimore: Williams and Wilkens, 1934.

Vaughan, Victor A. *A Doctor's Memories.* Indianapolis: Bobbs-Merrill, 1926.

Vaughn, Stephen. *Holding Fast the Inner Lines: Democracy, Nationalism, and the Committee on Public Information.* Chapel Hill: University of North Carolina Press, 1980.

Walworth, Arthur. *Woodrow Wilson.* Boston: Houghton Mifflin, 1965.

Unpublished Materials and Oral Histories

Fanning, Patricia J. "Disease and the Politics of Community: Norwood and the Great Flu Epidemic of 1918." PhD diss., Boston College, 1995.

Oral history of Clifford Adams, June 3, 1982, provided by Charles Hardy of West Chester University.

Pettit, Dorothy Ann. "A Cruel Wind: America Experiences the Pandemic Influenza, 1918–1920, A Social History." PhD diss., University of New Hampshire, 1976.

Wolper, Gregg. "The Origins of Public Diplomacy: Woodrow Wilson, George Creel, and the Committee on Public Information." PhD diss., University of Chicago, 1991.

ACKNOWLEDGMENTS

This book was initially supposed to be a straightforward story of the deadliest epidemic in human history, told from the perspectives of both scientists who tried to fight it and political leaders who tried to respond to it. I thought it would take me two and a half years to write, three at the most.

That plan didn't work. Instead this book took seven years to write. It has evolved (and, I hope, grown) into something rather different than originally conceived.

It took so long partly because it didn't seem possible to write about the scientists without exploring the nature of American medicine at this time, for the scientists in this book did far more than laboratory research. They changed the very nature of medicine in the United States.

And finding useful material on the epidemic proved remarkably difficult. It was easy enough to find stories of death, but my own interests have always focused on people who try to exercise some kind of control over events. Anyone doing so was far too busy, far too overwhelmed, to pay any attention to keeping records.

In the course of these seven years, many people helped me.

Some shared with me their own research or helped me find material, others helped me understand the influenza virus and the disease it causes, and some offered advice on the manuscript. None of them, of course, is responsible for any errors of commission or omission, whether factual or of judgment, in the book. (Wouldn't it be entertaining to once read an acknowledgment in which the author blames others for any mistakes?)

Two friends, Steven Rosenberg and Nicholas Restifo at the National Cancer Institute, helped me understand how a scientist approaches a problem and also read parts of the manuscript and offered comments. So did Peter Palese at the Icahn School of Medicine at Mount in New York, one of the world's leading experts on the influenza virus, who very generously gave his time and expertise. Robert Webster, at St. Jude Children's Research Hospital, like Palese a world leader in influenza research, offered his insights and criticisms as well. Ronald French checked the manuscript for accuracy on the clinical course of the disease. Vincent Morelli introduced me to Warren Summers, who, along with the entire pulmonary section of the Louisiana State University Health Sciences Center in New Orleans, helped me understand much of what happens in the lung during an influenza attack; Warren was extremely patient and repeatedly helpful. Mitchell Friedman at the Tulane University School of Medicine also explained events in the lung to me.

Jeffrey Taubenberger at the Armed Forces Institute of Pathology kept me abreast of his latest findings. John Yewdell at the National Institutes of Health also explained much about the virus. Robert Martensen at Tulane made valuable suggestions on the history of medicine. Alan Kraut at American University also read and commented on part of the manuscript.

I also particularly thank John McLachlan of the Tulane-Xavier Center for Bioenvironmental Research, who very much helped make this book possible. William Steinmann, head of the Center for Clinical Effectiveness and Life Support at the Tulane Medical Center, generously gave his office space, knowledge of disease, and friendship.

All of the above have MDs or PhDs or both. Without their assistance I would have been lost trying to understand my own cytokine storm.

People who write books are always thanking librarians and archivists. They have good reason to. Virtually everyone at the Rudolph Matas Library of the Health Sciences at Tulane University was extraordinarily helpful to me, but Patsy Copeland deserves truly special mention. So do Kathleen Puglia, Sue Dorsey, and Cindy Goldstein.

I also want to thank Mark Samels of WGBH's *American Experience*, who made available all the material collected for its program on the pandemic; Janice Goldblum at the National Academy of Sciences, who did more than just her job; Gretchen Worden at the Mutter Museum in Philadelphia; Jeffrey Anderson, then a graduate student at Rutgers, and Gary Gernhart, then a graduate student at American University, both of whom generously offered me their own research; Charles Hardy of West Chester University, who gave me oral histories he had collected;

and Mitch Yockelson at the National Archives, who gave me the benefit of his knowledge. Eliot Kaplan, then the editor of *Philadelphia Magazine*, also supported the project. I also want to thank Pauline Miner and Catherine Hart in Kansas. For help with photos, I want to especially thank Susan Robbins Watson at the American Red Cross, Lisa Pendergraff at the Dudley Township Library in Kansas, Andre Sobocinski and Jan Herman at the US Navy Bureau of Medicine and Surgery, Darwin Stapleton at the Rockefeller Archive Center, and Nancy McCall at the Alan Mason Chesney Medical Archives at Johns Hopkins. I also want to thank Pat Ward Friedman for her information about her grandfather.

Now we come to my editor, Wendy Wolf. Although this is only my fifth book, counting magazine articles I've worked with literally dozens of editors. Wendy Wolf very much stands out. She edits the old-fashioned way; she works at it. On this manuscript she worked particularly hard, and working with her has been a pleasure. It is a true statement to say that, for better or worse (and I hope better), this book wouldn't exist without her. I'd also like to thank Hilary Redmon for her diligence, reliability, and just general assistance.

Thanks also to my agent, Raphael Sagalyn, as good a professional as there is. I've had many editors but only one agent, a fact that speaks for itself.

Finally, I thank my brilliant wife, Margaret Anne Hudgins, who helped me in too many ways to enumerate, including both in concept and in the particular—but chiefly by being herself. And then there are the cousins.